M000164098

SCHIZOPHRENIA
DEFEATED

Printed and bound by Lightning Source,
Milton Keynes, U.K.

Published by Crossbridge Books
Tree Shadow, Berrow Green
Martley WR6 6PL
Tel: 01886 821128

© Crossbridge Books 2004

First published 2004.

All rights reserved. No part of this publication may be reproduced,
stored in a retrieval system, or transmitted in any form or by any
means – electronic, mechanical, photocopying, recording or
otherwise – without prior permission of the Copyright owner.

ISBN 0 9543573 4 5

British Library Cataloguing in Publication Data. A catalogue
record for this book is available from the British Library.

Also published by Crossbridge Books:

The God of Miracles Trevor and Anne Dearing
Stepping-Stone Miracles Des Morton

Total Healing Trevor Dearing (published by ***Mohr Books*** –
                              an imprint of Crossbridge Books)

SCHIZOPHRENIA DEFEATED

JAMES STACEY

CROSSBRIDGE BOOKS

Acknowledgements

Many thanks to Eileen Mohr, my publisher, for her willingness and faith to put in print an autobiography dealing with a very controversial subject; to Father-in-law Maurice for suggestions and corrections; to Bob Iles for help in printing the chapters in the early days of writing; and finally, and most importantly, to Tina for her enduring patience in releasing me over many hours to discharge the burden of writing in order to bring hope to thousands.

Dedication

This book is dedicated to the Lord Jesus Christ, who made my story of freedom possible; to two heaven-sent and unique wives, Pamela and Tina, whose inspired love, devotion and hope spoke into my seemingly hopeless condition. To my loving children, Alison and Philip, for their unfailing support during life in the wilderness. To late Mum Horton, their Grandma, for everything she meant to all of us. And to my father-in-law, Maurice Winterburn and his late wife, Esther, who supported Tina in her days of challenge to my life.

Biblical Quotations

are taken (unless otherwise indicated) from the
HOLY BIBLE, NEW INTERNATIONAL VERSION
Copyright © 1973, 1978, 1984 by International Bible Society.
Used by permission.

Contents

Preface

We were glued to the television screen with millions more around the world. There were some delays before Nelson Mandela appeared, walking as a free man after 26 years of imprisonment, but the moment the camera brought him to the screen stirred in me strong emotions of joy I shall never forget.

As I watched him walking in his new-found freedom from Robben Island, little did I realise that three months later I, too, would be stepping from a mental prison house which had kept me enslaved for exactly the same length of time as the solitary confinement endured by the leader of the African National Congress.

Though a Christian, my long-standing problem of schizophrenia had held me in a constant deep bondage. Nobody had been able to deal with the evil entrenched deeply in my life until that year.

Seeing Nelson Mandela obviously rejoicing that his long spell in prison was now over brought a real and definite hope of freedom into my spirit.

If you are suffering from the worst psychotic disorder of schizophrenia, or any form of mental bondage or problem, my story of freedom is sent out to bring hope through the power of prayer to secure release for you no matter how desperately it may be needed. If you are caring for a mentally sick relative, go forward with believing faith in God through Jesus Christ who opens up a way through and out of the problem.

I seek to honour the unbounded possibilities of prayer and glorify the ability of God to answer every need. My story demonstrates the unfailing love of God and how with Him all things are possible.

James Stacey
Founder of *Pray Until Schizophrenia Heals*
March 2004

1

Early days to teenage years

My childhood was typical of many belonging to the working-class born during the Second World War when families struggled to make ends meet. It was, however, full of happiness and normal boyish adventure, and looking back I still retain pleasant memories of my early years.

Living in a beautiful South Yorkshire village where everyone knew just about everybody else in our closely-knit community brought tremendous advantages as the youngest of three boys growing up together.

When my father returned home from serving in the War after being involved in the evacuation of Dunkirk, he secured a surface labouring job at a colliery five miles away. During primary school years and beyond, I seldom got close to him because of the long hours he was working in order to give us a basic standard of living.

He often arrived home so tired after cycling on a round trip of 10 miles to and from work in all weathers for his normal shift with regular overtime, and 16-hours' weekend work, that he had little enough energy to devote to us after dinner.

My brothers were five years and nearly three years older. Mother had wanted me to be a girl, which in itself seemed a natural and seemingly harmless desire, but this was to affect my life in a devastating way.

She herself had not started life ideally, when at the age of two, her father, aged 27, was killed underground in a roof fall at the Kiveton Park Colliery, near Sheffield at a time when her mother was expecting her sister.

1

Added to that early setback, she became unsettled in the following years when her mother remarried. Her new husband was a man from outside the village with children of his own. My grandmother died at the age of 42, when mother was 12, and she and her sister were forced to live with different relations. Auntie was fortunate to get the better of the arrangement, going to stay with an aunt and uncle who had lost their only child and found her a lovely replacement.

My mother, however, could only be found a home with her grandmother in the same village. She, at the age of 51, had already brought up seven children of her own and wanted life easier.

The circumstances my mother encountered brought rejection into her life, which sadly was to remain until her death in 1995. Growing up she felt insecure and lacked the warmth and love of a stable home. There was no alternative but for her to enter "service" as a teenager, waiting on a family at a large house. She later moved to a Nottinghamshire village, employed at a large hall in similar work while coming under the care of an auntie. Life was plagued by rejection and this affected her so greatly that the condition later transferred itself to me in the womb, leading to schizophrenia and a 26-year-long struggle for survival.

My life in the early years spent in a two-up and two-down end terrace house was enjoyable, though I was unaware of the great sacrifice my father was putting in for us all.

My brothers gained entrance from our local junior school to the well-known Woodhouse Grammar School in east Sheffield. When I failed the examination to go there I felt like the black sheep of the family.

I had not got their grasp of ideas and mastery of subjects, and while I excelled at sports, being chosen to captain the junior school football team, I lacked their ability to succeed in lessons. In years to come I was to reflect on this and other shortcomings in the mental realm, which suggested to me what could have been the early undetected signs of schizophrenia before the illness revealed itself in "full bloom."

During these years of my childhood development, my mother worked tremendously hard in caring for us, but at the same time there was always the worrying side to her, and the absence of

spontaneous joy. I would often return home early from Sunday School and wonder why I was an intrusion as she was busy with housework.

Everyone knew Mum to be a hard worker, and how she always managed to turn all three of us out at the annual Sunday School anniversary in a complete new rig-out was an amazing feat. She took pride in her three boys, quietly rejoiced over their successes and only wanted the best for them. But there was an inability to express her emotions freely because of the scars and wounds of rejection still affecting her.

Any lack of emotional strength being poured into my life, though, was compensated for in a wonderful way because just down the gennel from where we lived was a friendly school caretaker and his wife, Mr and Mrs Bill Lynch. Having no children of their own, they both befriended and loved me, and made me feel very special.

From the earliest memory of four or so, I was made to feel welcome at their home. I loved helping Mr Lynch tidy the garden, and received regular treats to watch Barnsley Football Club play home matches, equalled by the frequent excitement of weekend trips to a Lincolnshire farm to load the boot of the Morris 8 with tray upon tray of eggs.

These were for delivery on the milk round Mrs Lynch owned. Every trip was followed by the anticipated thrill of calling at our favourite café for afternoon tea.

It was Mr Lynch's dream that one day I would play cricket for Yorkshire, so at a very early age he would position me in front of the garden gate and coach me how to play a straight bat to his underarm bowls. The interest he showed in my life was a great joy.

When he promised to turn up at the school football game on his way home from work on a Saturday morning, I would keep one eye on the game and the other on the welfare entrance awaiting his arrival on motorcycle.

Every day I would visit them, and their house soon became my second home. Mrs Lynch would always do a little extra dinner for me when her husband returned home from work.

I would sit on the steps outside the front door watching for him to turn the corner up the road near the parish church, and then give the signal for dinner to be served. The memory of sitting with them,

tucking into potatoes mashed with butter and milk and covered in meat and rich gravy, always followed by sweet courses, I remember with delight.

I was unaware at the time just how much input they were having into my life. I can never remember a quarrel between them, though as the years went by I was sometimes amused when they came to settle their accounts with each other in respect of acquiring the eggs.

Mr Lynch's unfailing question: "Now how much do you owe me for the petrol in fetching the eggs from the farm?" was a routine which caused a chuckle in my young heart.

Mr Lynch would often make up stories that were a real joy, and even read to me. I used to take my old case full of a young boy's treasures down to their house and find great delight in getting everything out: toys; Meccano sets; cards; and the few books I owned.

I soon developed a good memory, boasting at one stage of being able to recite the forty-eight states of America by categorising them according to first letters. I regularly succeeded in the annual Scripture examination at our local chapel and was able to remember Bible stories fairly easily. On the first Sunday in May, I would recite from high up on the anniversary platform to the joy and delight of Mum seated in the middle of the congregation.

The acquisition of a good memory was to prove of immense value in years to come when the illness of schizophrenia was to take a grip on my life. There followed very strong suggestions of suicide — but having memorised the Bible I was able to ward off these attacks as the Scriptures became a real lifeline of strength in the fight to survive.

Having failed my eleven plus, I proceeded to go to a Secondary Modern school in the next village, during the course of which I again failed to secure a spare place at Woodhouse Grammar School which was open to a few students. I then went to the adjacent Secondary Technical School, choosing to complete a three-year commercial course in preference to metalwork or woodwork, which the majority of my friends chose to follow.

At this time I was 13 years old. Before going to school I delivered 120 newspapers, covering about half the village of South Anston where I lived, and about thirty spread over the same area at night.

In the commercial class I was one of four boys heavily outnumbered by 26 girls. I enjoyed shorthand, typing and even grew to like book-keeping, but struggled with other subjects mainly because, so I thought at the time, they were either poorly put across or taught by teachers who were less than winsome.

In retrospect, I just wonder how much my thinking processes were affected by schizophrenia lying dormant in my life. While I went on to write shorthand faster than my three pals, and before leaving school was only one of three in the whole class to pass 100 words per minute in RSA examinations, I struggled with mastering the positions of outlines and the basics of the skill. What pulled me through exams was nothing less than the ability to memorise the outlines irrespective of which position they occupied, whether above, on, or below the line.

I also found difficulty mastering the basics in six months of learning to play the piano, and used to envy those who could get the timing right. The subject of Algebra caused many problems, but my classmates often rescued me. On a memorable occasion, I was given a helping hand in the changing-rooms after a sports lesson to complete the previous night's homework — and then crept gingerly into the headmaster's study to slip my book on the opened pile on his desk.

Along with my brothers I regularly attended Sunday School. As often happens in teenage life, they both drifted away. I was consciously asking myself certain questions on seeing their departure and wondered if I ought to finish too. Surely there could be nothing in it, or else the appeal of church would have held their interest!

At the age of 14, when I was undecided just what to do, the greatest moment in my life occurred — starting a relationship with Jesus Christ. I thought Christ could be received anytime, anywhere, or at least that was the reasoning in my heart when one Saturday evening I attended a Youth for Christ film in an evangelistic meeting six miles away from home in the Gaiety Theatre, Worksop. During an appeal to receive Christ, the convicting power of the Holy Spirit so arrested and disturbed me that I found myself broken before God who, I recognised, had sent His Son to die for me. It was an encounter which brought the living presence of Jesus into my life,

without which I now know I would have been unable to face the years that followed.

How grateful I am today for that life-changing moment as a young teenager this side of suffering the most severe psychotic disorder of all. Although it was to play havoc for more than a third of the average life span from my early twenties, it was the same mighty power of Jesus working in my life which would finally defeat the terrible, evil darkness of schizophrenia.

2

The illness dawned on my life

In the summer of 1958 I left school with the definite desire of wanting to be a journalist, though I had not pursued an opening at the time of leaving. I started work in the middle of a heatwave at a steel and wire works in the next village, but felt confined in the small warehouse where I typed invoices.

I was grateful to my former Sunday School superintendent, Mr William Hogg, head of wages, for securing me the job; but within a few months I felt unfulfilled and wanted to try my hand at journalism. A schoolfriend, John Sadler, had landed a reporter's job on the *South Yorkshire Times*, the same weekly where the famous broadcaster-journalist, Michael Parkinson had begun his career. I decided to pursue a similar opening.

On a cold wintry night, I travelled to an unfamiliar part of South Yorkshire to the head office at Mexborough to see the Editor, Mr Sidney Hacking. After testing me out with questions and checking my shorthand note, he gave me a job — to start on 9th February, 1959, working two days on the *Woodhouse Express* based in Darnall, in the east end of Sheffield and four days on the *Rotherham Express*.

It was a job I immediately liked. The encouragement of my school shorthand-typist teacher Mrs Moran, whom I loved more than any other teacher for her humaneness and fun, that I would make a good reporter, had gone a long way in motivating me.

My first mentor was Tony Hardisty, later to go to the *Sunday Express*. The first story he picked up, with me sitting on the back of the firm's scooter, was of a car accident on the main A57 just outside the grammar school village of Woodhouse, which eventually was to become my patch for local news.

The regular weekly routine was to visit certain well-known local figures, such as the vicar and other church ministers, frequent notable haunts of local workingmen's clubs and public houses for homing society news and snooker results, and gather the unalterable paragraph of who spoke at certain meetings of the Salvation Army. I was instructed never to miss obtaining the winners of this beetle drive and that whist drive — all tedious stuff it was to prove, but the kind of things that sell local papers.

This routine of reporting village events was pleasantly contrasted by the greater challenge of learning the job in the heart of Rotherham where there was such a variety of news to gather, though again I had a village outside town to cover in common with the other reporters.

I revelled in the type of jobs which might find me court reporting on a Monday; sitting in the Civic Theatre on a Tuesday struggling to find inspiration to critique a play or local operatic performance; attending an inquest or Council meeting on Wednesday, and the promise of a free seat in the press box at Millmoor on Saturday to report the fortunes of Rotherham United. Our office secured orders on a lineage basis for match reports from some Sunday nationals, and Saturday evening sports papers circulated in the area of the visiting team.

It was as varied a job as one could obtain, allowing a freedom unsurpassed. I never possessed any career plan in journalism in working out how long to remain on the paper. The fact that I was serving three-year indentures brought with it a commitment to attend a Thursday afternoon journalist school, which for the most part I abandoned for a trip to the pictures or for a lazy afternoon in the park.

I still found studying and application to study quite a difficult pursuit, as had been the case in the years preparing for GCE examinations at school. Woven into this problem, I do believe, was a difficulty in the subconscious related in some way to the illness which was to steal over my life at 22. It also manifested itself in an inability to write as freely as I would have wished, even in the realm of reporting football matches — a sport I loved and could relate to.

As time progressed, I found myself second-in-command of the *Woodhouse Express*, and assumed control of the office when my colleague was on holiday. I had a good news sense, and would go to any lengths to get a good story. When it was the kind that had an appeal for the nationals, I would seize it with both hands and do the rounds with transfer charge calls to the Manchester editions in the hope of securing extra cash if the story appeared.

In the final months of serving my indentures, I became a little restless and was beginning to feel the need for a change, though I cherished no immediate attraction for securing a job on the evening paper in Sheffield. But something else was stirring in my life. I was beginning to take my faith in Jesus Christ more seriously. The drawing power of the Holy Spirit was causing me to ask deeper questions.

It was in the early summer of 1962 when a mention of a television programme showing the life of a Methodist Lay Training Home, Cliff College at Calver, near Sheffield, caught my interest. I purposely kept away from church that night to find out what was on offer.

During the programme, three students were interviewed and spoke of their faith in Jesus Christ in a deeper way than I knew. I found myself stirred by their testimonies and desired to attend such a college. I mentioned to my likeable Methodist minister, the Rev Geoffrey Hawkridge, that I had been very impressed with the programme.

His immediate question was, "Would you like to go to Cliff?"

I said, "Yes" — and in a matter of days the application was received, filled in, and I had a place reserved as a student to begin a one-year course starting in the autumn.

There was a temptation to stay on the paper, for precisely at the same time as securing a place at the College came the offer of promotion to be in charge of the Hoyland edition near Barnsley. But my heart was set on leaving, and I had no regrets in serving my notice followed by a hastily arranged two-week scooter holiday in the South of France before starting my studies in September.

Being away from home for the very first time was an experience I soon overcame. Cliff was to become my spiritual home, and in that year I met some wonderful men desirous of serving God either going into full-time Christian ministry, or returning to their normal

9

occupation on completing the course.

Upon reflection, I have come to believe that the latent illness of schizophrenia was stirred in some measure during this year, as a desire to go deeper with Christ gripped my life.

Simultaneously, a strange passivity hung over my life which the Principal, Tom Meadley, had commented on. During the lectures I appeared to him not to be listening or grasping the import of what was being taught on theology, and the growing passivity which was to become a feature of my life in years to come was something he had discerned.

When I asked for permission to be allowed to journey about 20 miles or so to play football with my team, Anston Miners Welfare, just inside the South Yorkshire border, he greeted me as I walked into his study, with the words, "Are you still as dormant as ever?"

At the time I deeply resented his words, but later concluded that what he had discerned had been correct. It is my firm belief that the demon of schizophrenia, located in my soul, seeing my determination to follow Christ, was stirred during my days at College, but the full emergence of the illness was yet to come.

On completing the course I returned home to continue studying, having a desire to enter the Methodist ministry but with no definite long-term preparation plans in mind. My immediate goal was to secure acceptance as a local preacher and pass the examinations. I was involved in freelance journalism in a small way at the same time to help pay for my keep at home.

The eight months, between September 1963 and April 1964, contained days of quiet waiting on God in my bedroom without any audible prayer as I genuinely struggled to get to know God in a deeper way. The complications and frustrations experienced within were strangely caused by the fact that at the same time God was working in my spirit, something evil was stirring deep inside my soul life. It was the schizophrenic "presence", and was shortly to emerge.

I just couldn't put my finger on the problem why it was taking so long for my spiritual thirst to be satisfied. I didn't at that time possess any teaching about the body, soul and spirit which later on became so precious, needful and helpful. Although I realised that my quest involved God coming into me rather than striving to move into God, the lack of progress brought weariness and a withdrawn

passivity.

Then an experience happened in the spring of 1964 of the precious baptism of the Holy Spirit, which was both wonderfully joyous and powerful. During a visit for fellowship to an elderly, frail widow named Mrs Fawcett, God broke through in mighty power as we prayed together.

"Shall we have our usual time of prayer before I leave?" I asked.

"Of course," she replied.

I knelt down by the heavy armchair and began praising God from my heart for what must have been several minutes, when the Holy Spirit filled the room. I had never before experienced such delight in God. Love and joy tangibly washed over us and we were aglow with the warmth of the glory of God.

On entering the kitchen at home, my mother noticed straight away that I looked different. She exclaimed:

"What's the matter with your face?"

I asked: "What *is* the matter with my face?"

She replied: "It's glowing!"

I went upstairs out of interest to look in the bathroom mirror. There was a radiance on my face of which I had been unaware. Though God had wonderfully met with us, I couldn't handle, never mind assess correctly, what happened in the room at the flat that night. While the power and joy of the Holy Spirit were continuously present for many weeks, the encounter stirred the "opposing presence" of schizophrenia already resident in my soul life.

It seemed ironic, in retrospect, that such a momentous encounter like this which, for another Christian without my condition, might be the springboard to deeper life and new things in God, conversely brought deeper and more embroiled complications in the mental realm through the birth of a psychotic disorder.

I eventually began to lose control of my life, thought I was somebody special because of what had happened, and was unable to realise that the resultant delusions which occurred gave entrance to a religious spirit into my life alongside the ruling spirit of schizophrenia already there.

I did strange things at that time when I had untiring energy, boldness and a misguided zeal. A simple desire to open the church at midnight for prayer should not normally be a problem, but on one

occasion it resulted in friction with a chapel trustee.

I actually went to his house, having been refused the key by the caretaker, and asked:

"May I have the key to open the church for prayer? I want to get people into church to pray."

"It's rather late to be doing that, isn't it?" he replied.

Recognising that I wasn't my normal self, he refused and fetched my father to take me home.

At this time I came under the care of the local doctor and started the first of many visits over the years to psychiatrists in Sheffield and Chesterfield. During the first visit I was told that I had suffered a mild nervous breakdown and was prescribed short-term largactil tablet treatment. The days that followed brought increased complexity concerning what I knew, or rather what I did not know about myself, together with a withdrawn and quiet existence altogether different from the side I had known earlier in my life.

I returned to the College soon afterwards for the first time after my student year had finished, for the customary well-supported Whitsuntide Anniversary celebrations. I took with me a copy of Karl Barth's *Evangelical Theology*, and gave it to Principal Meadley for the College library in appreciation of the year at Cliff.

Dr Skevington Wood, who was later to become a lecturer and Principal, and a great personal help, had been addressing the crowds on the story of the prodigal son. The general tenor of my excited mind can be judged when, mixing with a group of people who were firing questions at him, I chipped in, "Is it possible for a person to receive the gift of the Holy Spirit and not know it?" A strange question to ask indeed. Before he could answer, I asked him to preach on it at the next meeting.

I soon applied to my former newspaper for my old job back as a reporter and was readily taken on — it almost seemed they would love to have me return. The appointment this time was at the head office in Mexborough, working in an atmosphere and setting a little different from former years in the east end of Sheffield and Rotherham.

But the staff of the paper whom I had known very well over the years soon began to notice a change in me which was attributable to

something more than my having been away from the job for two years. I was preoccupied with a mental problem they had no idea I was carrying, a condition which was to get worse in the months to follow and result in having my job terminated.

I was sent out three times in the early days of restarting to get the details of a fire at a haulage firm, because the important and essential facts were missing. I overheard a comment poking fun at me over the incident. I never even called at the firm, relying on details for my report from an evening newspaper. I seemed unrelated to a job which before I had loved and thought, along with others, that I was good at doing.

I lived in lodgings at a private address in Mexborough when I began the appointment, but the days were lonely and unhappy and I never mustered the old enthusiasm for the job. Although there was a "well done" for getting a good story now and again or providing more news from an area that had been recently available from another reporter, it seemed as though the work was more difficult to perform. Constantly tired through taking largactil tablets, I showed evidence of dragging my feet.

By the spring of 1965 I was travelling the 15 or so miles to work and back by scooter from my parents' home in North Anston. I continued experiencing a restlessness in my life and a dissatisfaction which presented a burden. The daily habit of prayer in which I asked God for strength to meet the demands of life was the only means of seeking help to survive. Sure enough the Lord was honouring my seeking Him but I had no idea that there were evil presences* living within my life. This growing nest of spirits imposed restrictions on my freedom in the mental realm. Far more seriously, as I was to find out, they were bent on destroying me.

In the midst of all this confusion of darkness in my soul, God never stopped drawing me to Himself. Though I was fighting a hidden foe at that time undiscerned, and would have been even more ignorant of the means to evict it, I determined with all my heart to follow the Saviour I had come to love. I even prayed, with something of a fighting spirit, resolving to battle on in spite of my condition: "Lord, I don't care what it costs, I want to go deeper with you."

Little did I realise that I was exerting too much effort and

determination. I genuinely thought that to go deeper meant a continual striving. But this, I now believe and know, was being caused by the evil spirits within, and God was not responsible for this. I suppose I had done in faith all that a believer has to do in order to enthrone Christ at the centre of life, but the restlessness within persuaded me to try to do more.

*Note:

If you, the reader, feel inclined to reject the idea of the existence of evil spirits, please bear with me until you have read my story; then make your judgement.

3

The battle raged to destroy me

It was in the summer of 1965 that the battle for my mind reached its peak. It is impossible to communicate the sheer hell endured over several weeks. Looking back, I thank God for His protection, knowing He was mindful of all that I was going through, and would only allow satan and his forces to go so far.

In the midst of this mental trauma, I began seeking the mind of Christ, believing that it was given through interceding for others. I decided to spend an hour of my one-and-a-half hour dinner break in the parish church at Mexborough seeking God for this gift as I prayed for people, particularly members of my family.

Such times of seeking God diligently were rewarded and inspired me to continue. Satan knew I was serious in my pursuit of God and he began to implement a strategy to prevent it.

Another experience happened when the presence of the Holy Spirit drew near. The "evil presence" in my life at this time was now not only stirred but retaliated in bombarding my inner life and mind with strong proposals of suicide that were aimed at destroying me.

It was a beautifully bright summer's morning when, having arrived early for work, I walked beside the river close to the railway station and only a few minutes away from the newspaper office. What a glorious encounter of the glory of God saturated my life as I soaked in the natural sunshine. I was not praying aloud, simply worshipping the Lord when His Presence seemed to be everywhere in such power and glory. Again, I didn't know how to handle this encounter with God. If it occurred today I would be lost in worship and inspired to humility, but I walked to the office strangely seeking a reason for what had happened and desiring the "wonderful feeling"

to continue. In a short space of time there was a spiritual attack on my life, soon leading to depression and passivity, because the touch of the Holy Spirit had again stirred up an evil presence in my soul.

Walking the streets and travelling on the bus in the course of my work, an overwhelming bondage began to grip my mind. I couldn't concentrate properly and was moving about in inner confusion. I fought to shake off the immense dark cloud wrapped around my thoughts, though it never occurred to me that the presence of evil spirits was the cause, and that I ought to have pleaded the blood of Jesus.

The last night at work, before my mental condition was to become serious, saw me seated at the typewriter unable to put together a simple church paragraph about scouts holding a jumble sale. My mind was virtually paralysed and unable to function. With extreme difficulty I managed to type the news, but not before everyone had left, one of them, obviously observing my condition but giving no help, saying, "Jim looks as though he's going to be here a lot longer." I was the last to leave the office that night, feeling like someone on his own in the middle of a desert crying out for help.

It was impossible to return to work in this condition. Neither could I fulfil preaching appointments "on trial" in the Methodist Church on the Sundays that followed. The attacks on my mind intensified so much that I eventually needed to stay in bed. I had no medication and was bombarded relentlessly with evil thoughts. I sank into passivity as all resistance left me. It seemed as though the floodgates of hell had been unleashed into my mind. On one occasion I felt as though my whole body was stretched out in the lower part of a ship and I was fighting for life as thick slime and sludge covered me.

My parents were not aware of the seriousness of my condition, neither were my brothers, who were also living at home, though the doctor's note I kept receiving said my illness was schizophrenia. But unknown to me help was on the way. A doctor urgently summoned by my favourite aunt suddenly appeared in my bedroom and injected me, hoping it would put me to sleep (an amount I later heard it said was enough to put an elephant out).

Next, an ambulance pulled up outside and I was strapped into a chair, carried downstairs and lifted into the vehicle. A strong sense of fear gripped me when the siren sounded as we moved off, and I began fighting in the ambulance with my father and the attendant as I was so afraid. The journey over 14 miles to the old and formidable Victorian Middlewood Sanatorium Hospital in Sheffield was a literal nightmare, made worse by the fact that I couldn't understand what was happening. The windows were half clear and half dark, which made me even more confused.

I then remember half-waking up naked in a cell-like room on my own, sprawled out on the floor without any covering. It seemed as though I had remained there for ages, resenting the smell of my own urine, until the Charge Nurse unlocked the door and talked down at me without getting any response:

"So, you're James Stacey?"

I was detained at the hospital a few weeks, receiving electric shock treatment and medication. Taking exercise in the foreground of the hospital with inmates carrying deep psychiatric problems, I kept saying to myself, "What on earth are you doing here, Jim? You're not as bad as these fellas."

During my time on Ward 11, I succumbed to the electric shock treatment which I received without any resistance. The effects of these shocks, plus the numerous largactil tablets I was taking, made me feel as though my head was definitely not a part of me. Even in this first of many real confinements I remember trusting in God and praying for help. At this time, the word of God was not as real to me as it later became, but nevertheless I saw the need to keep faith in the Lord at all costs.

After being discharged from the hospital, I returned home for weeks of recuperation, and eventually felt fit enough to go back to work. Though the editor showed a certain reluctance for me to start, his compassion shone through when I remarked that I didn't know any other kind of work. I was on tranquillisers at the time and remained on them for months, though the effects created constant tiredness for me. I kept my job going for six or seven months with great difficulty as the illness became more and more entrenched in my life.

Struggling through day to day with schizophrenia was bad enough in itself but to contend with the added onslaught of a

17

religious spirit driving, aiding and abetting a confused mind, made my condition much worse. Delusions appeared to be so real, and I seemed propelled to pursue them. The first of many occurred when, utterly confused and restless, I hired a taxi for over 20 miles to travel to Cliff College where I just had to see the Principal, the Rev Howard Belben.

He was travelling back from Manchester when I arrived an hour before midnight. Although I rang the bell, my entering the house caused concern to Mrs Belben. I decided to wait for him in the college dining room and heard him walking down the corridor just before one o'clock. He listened to what I had to say, then promptly escorted me to a bedroom, armed with clean linen.

Throughout the night, I didn't even get into bed, since my mind was alive and excited and "on the move". Mentally disturbed, I would follow a thought as soon as it came into my mind, as happened when I went into the college chapel at about four in the morning and struck up "Blessed Assurance" at full blast on the organ. Appearing in the dining room at breakfast, I rightly received disapproval for the racket from a student who that morning had hoped to have had a good night's sleep in readiness for a ministerial interview.

Escorted by members of the college staff, evangelist Norman Smith, who had been my team leader in summer mission treks while at the college, and administrative officer Alan Stapleton, I was driven by car to the newspaper office.

I lost my job that day because it was obvious to the staff that I was suffering in mind and had become something of an embarrassment to them. As always, the editor, Mr Hacking, was understanding and courteous, and wrote me a reference, suggesting that I might find a sedentary job which would have less taxing commitment on my life.

I eventually finished up in Middlewood Hospital again. The Rev Belben visited me and found me in a cot with the sides up when he called at Ward 11. I had just received electric shock treatment and was thoroughly unaware of his presence. I was disturbed from deep sleep and sheer mental fatigue after the treatment and was told:

"There's a visitor to see you."

With difficulty I opened my eyes, and though I recognised him I didn't say a word, but went straight back to sleep. Quite a long journey of around 30 miles for such a brief pastoral call. But as I told him later, "It didn't mean much to me at the time, but it certainly does now."

There would have been a lot of difficulty coping with life at that time, and subsequently, but for the fact that during my latest spell on the paper I had fallen in love with the sweetest of women with a Christ-like quiet spirit, who was always there to support me.

Pam Horton was a radiant Pentecostal believer who used to ring church news through to the paper. I had made it known that I was interested in what she was reporting as a genuine born-again believer. When I began covering the area where she worked in the clerk's office at Dearne Urban Council our paths eventually crossed. I was attracted by her beautiful looks. She had brown sparkling eyes, and lovely chestnut brown hair. I made any excuse to call regularly at her office on the pretext of seeking news. I even began to look forward to reporting the housing committee's monthly meeting, knowing she would be in attendance taking the minutes.

I determined to ask her home for tea followed by attending church. She had to go downstairs to the reception on a day I was in her office and I knew this was the moment to issue the invitation. I soon followed her through the door and found her standing behind the desk sorting papers.

"Would you like to come and have tea at home and then we could drop in at our local church?" I blurted out. I had caught her on one leg.

"Er, yes. That would be fine," she replied.

On the day in question, I arrived outside Winterwell Road Pentecostal Church, West Melton, near Rotherham on my 125cc Vespa scooter. When Pam came out after completing her teaching in Sunday School, I was treated to an entourage of inquisitive interest from fellow teachers vying for space on the church steps. Everyone was smiling as Pam struggled to fasten her "bumblebee" type helmet. We were waved off with a mixture of delight and curiosity as her friends wondered if I might be the answer to their prayers.

During another spell in the Sanatorium, Pam stood by me and in

19

a lovely letter gave me cause for hope by saying that the present problem would not last and we had a lovely future ahead of us. She had prayed about our relationship in the light of knowing that I had schizophrenia — a fact not known by myself.

"I got the go-ahead for our marriage," she wrote, "by presenting you to the Lord in much the same way that Abraham presented Isaac on the altar. I desired only the will of God. The answer to that prayer came when the Lord gave you back to me, and then I knew it was right to proceed."

However, talking the matter over with her mother, she was told:

"It's not going to be easy, love, living with someone with that difficult condition."

We were deeply in love with each other. We were engaged in October 1966 and married on Easter Saturday 1967. She was definitely heaven's choice!

We began our married life in a terrace house at Wath-on-Dearne, near Rotherham, bought from our Pentecostal church. I worked as engineer's clerk at the local colliery about a mile away where I used to start work at 08.24. The discipline introduced to me at College of rising at 06.15 in order to pray stayed with me and the benefits received there helped me keep up the practice. I used to get up at that time for work and spend a good hour or so poring over the Scriptures.

Believing that if ever I was to abide in Christ, I must allow the word of God into my heart and perform what Jesus says in John, Chapter15, I determined to get out of bed early every morning even in the winter, before setting off for work. I would first of all make the coal fire and then have my quiet time. Waiting for the fire to start burning, I would sit in the kitchen with my Bible in my hands warming myself from the heater on the electric cooker.

During the first year of marriage, I was gripped by a desire to know God better, while being unable to recognise at the same time a strong oppression and the lack of deep rest within. The religious spirit was uniting forces with the schizophrenic demon and they proved formidable foes, as the years ahead were to prove. Although I enjoyed certain revelation from God's word, this religious spirit sought to distort a true interpretation to my mind, thereby aiding and abetting the schizophrenic demon. But reading the Bible nevertheless imparted strength to my heart and helped me to survive each day, a fact I did not fully appreciate.

Contemplating the Scriptures unlocked the key of meditation as flashes of inspiration by the Holy Spirit supplied truth at crucial moments of assault. But for these breakthroughs of truth in my spirit and to a mind that was not free I would not at that time, nor in the many years to come, have had the ability to persevere in prayer.

It never occurred to me that in seeking the deeper life of God which I so desired, that I was being hindered in that search by demonic forces. I was unaware of the concern I was proving to Pam in my daily life. She kept loving me and was committed in marriage no matter what happened.

We were to have 14 years of marriage together, and care for two lovely children. When I became free in years to come, I reflected on what she endured in her care of me and the triumph of her faith and patience. I have wept tears of joy to God for her, thanked Him for providing not just a wife but a heaven-sent choice who showed me endless love and devotion.

Our marriage suffered basically because I was not free. This affected every area of our relationship, sad to say. My preoccupation with myself, the inability to be both natural and normal, and the unpredictable mood swings were all part of everyday life. I could not, for example, perform the easiest of jobs around the house due to the thought of doing the job being a greater problem than the job itself.

The frustration Pam must have felt continuously by my lack of productivity and freedom to give an expected helping hand proved a real test of patience for her. It was as though my movements were all locked up in a body that refused to respond.

I began struggling with Romans chapters 6 to 8, memorising the Scriptures which were later to become so important to me in the fight to keep free against constant attacks by demons. In the far distant future I was to receive power and authority from God's word in using the name of Jesus to defeat and exorcise demons from my life.

The Lord pressed home the wonderful revelation in those days that if I was to be free then it meant knowing His inner abiding presence in my life in power. If through conscious faith I could retain the words in my heart, then that would be the answer.

21

Little did I realise the great significance of seeking and desiring the Lord to fill my heart with His thoughts — thoughts which the Psalmist assured me were as many as the sand on the seashore. If to be free in Jesus meant anything at all, it meant being free in the thought realm. Freedom from worry, defeat, despair, even frustration — a freedom I sought for my heart while struggling with a mind entrenched in bondage.

In the months that followed I struggled to know what it meant to live with the law of the spirit of life in Christ Jesus operating in my life. The issue of standing fast in the liberty with which Christ could make me free was revealed to me and became no half-hearted interest in daily living. The discovery of it I made mention of in a sermon lasting 50 minutes on freedom at our Pentecostal church.

I stressed among friends the importance of standing fast rather too much. Of course they were unaware of the increasing opposition in my life from satan and of the necessity for me to grasp hold of this truth as something absolutely essential. I was battling day in and day out with an evil psychotic disorder I did not fully appreciate, and must have appeared somewhat of an enigma to those who were close to me.

My need to rely more on God became more important, and I began to start praying in the evening in my bedroom, going over the next day's work. Travelling in my thoughts for over half an hour just on the journey to work alone, became a regular routine.

Pam would often find me upstairs when my time should have been hers. It was not that I was shut away all that time praying for others. My whole reason for being there centred on being preoccupied with fighting to keep alive and keeping up a habit which, although it seemed over the top to others, was vitally necessary to me to survive.

There were times when, through the Holy Spirit revealing Himself more to me and drawing closer, I thought the routine of praying in this way to be too meticulous and unnecessary. I began keeping a diary in which I wrote to give me guidance for the future. I put in it that meeting God in the morning ought to give me strength and resources to go out into the day.

Drawing on His power moment by moment should have made this practice of labouring over each particular detail a waste of time,

I thought.. I ought to be able, having prepared my heart in prayer in the morning, to trust God for whatever came my way and rejoice in the freedom He had given to me.

But this confusion in my thinking showed nothing less than the schizophrenic pattern of living with which I was battling. In my more lucid moments, the Holy Spirit was guiding me to do one thing; when the demonic forces inside me were fully at play, my line of thinking was challenged. The problem was that this struggle in the mind was a real drain, manifesting itself more and more in a withdrawn passivity.

My illness began to show itself in not being able to respond to do things without preparation. The ability to switch from one job to another was something I was beginning to find difficult to handle. My body became locked up in a straitjacket, the shackles of which were to tighten up and get stronger as the years went by. It became such a prison house that I thought to pray earnestly was to clasp my hands as tightly as possible, sometimes leaving indentations on them through the intensity of having gripped them so hard.

As the months went by I was all the time repeating over and over in my heart the word of God, very often at a pace too quick for normal thinking, but this was because of the lack of real freedom in bodily movement. I must have been a real drain on Pam, but she was always immensely patient and her strong faith carried her through. I couldn't see myself as she, and others, could see me; but, of course, that is just one of the limitations of schizophrenic life.

When I first began my job at Wath Colliery, I seemed to quickly settle into the routine of the duties as engineer's clerk and complete the work as soon as it came in. There was a certain thrill of accomplishment in being up-to-date and often ahead in preparing weekly lists of men working over the weekend. I kept holding my own ground, so to speak, though my freedom was certainly limited and my productivity reduced.

Prayer was maintained, but it seemed that all my efforts to perform it left no energy for anything else. So all-absorbing was the interest with myself that I would now never engage in prayer for others simply because I could never surmount my own difficulties so as to feel free to give them the necessary consideration.

An unending struggle went on inside me, and what was being

perpetually stirred needed prayerful resistance, demanding all my powers of mind and heart. So there was little left to devote to duties at work. The excessive preoccupation with self was daily and momentary. There was no letting up. Little did I realise at the time that it was satan's intention to wear me out so that he could destroy me.

The demon-possession taking hold of my life could be likened to ivy climbing up the trunk of a tree. The ivy, so I understand, is not sufficient to strangle the life of the tree but it reaches that same goal as it spreads itself around the tree, drawing the sap from the life of the tree. The size of the tree is gradually diminished as the ivy brings a heavy weight on the branches and finally wins the day.

The slowness with jobs at home was also apparent. While on the largactil tablets, I used to want to sleep after Sunday lunch. When I volunteered to do the washing up, it could take an hour and a quarter to finish everything. Handling and cleaning a lot of objects at one time called for a lot of energy, so much so that to break the monotony of the duty I would prop up a book in the window sill and "travel" at a snail's pace.

Throughout our marriage, I felt strengthened through the companionship and support of Pam, and I did my best to be a good husband, but my inner struggle for freedom continued and produced a dissatisfaction within.

There seemed to be a missing piece somewhere while knowing deep within that God alone was the answer. I was still unaware of the very real presence of demonic forces in my life, and of my own basic condition of schizophrenia.

This key demon worked tirelessly to attract other spirits into the nest of spirits now taking up residence in my life. The desire for the Lord was still there and the discipline of early morning prayer became established. In the Pentecostal church we attended, I preached regularly, though sometimes using other preachers' material. I thought I was beginning to see what it meant to walk in the spirit through the freedom of Christ, though I was a long way off the experience because of mental bondage.

With Pam on our Wedding Day, 1967

4

Struggling with bereavement

An unpleasant happening in the summer of 1968 had a gigantic effect on my life, taking me into a deeper psychotic disorder. While at work, someone spoke so harshly without provocation that I was more than upset by it. The criticism, which I should have been able to brush aside, caused me to go on the defensive and resolve that I would never allow anyone to speak to me like that again. So I started repeating Scriptures ten to the dozen in my heart as a kind of shield.

While scripturally sound, this method of so-called preservation brought problems when the already indwelling religious spirit deluded me into taking the practice too far. Soon I was unable to think normally to do my work, and productivity was adversely affected. My mind became so paralysed at times by fear that I was often rooted to the spot, once having to stay in a dark entry porch sitting on a cupboard for 45 minutes in the pit-yard building when I had left the office to go home.

Evil spirits of fear had begun to link themselves to the existing nest of spirits within my life. Though I had no knowledge of such things at the time, I now recall that the further trouble I was about to go through occurred when the demon of suicide gained entrance. The only way I was able to ward off this attack without casting it out was through the power of speaking in other tongues, which kept the tremendous onslaughts at bay, though the demon was to reappear many times suggesting I end my life.

Such an incident occurred on a day we had planned to take our new daughter Alison to see her grandmother just over half a mile

away in the same village. I had been held in an uncomfortable powerful bondage which I could neither talk about nor shake off. It was the first real experience of many that were to follow in which I felt that my whole life was threatened from within by forces seeking to destroy me.

As I pushed the pram there was hardly any conversation between Pam and myself because of a mounting desperation coming over me. It became absolutely necessary to do something. As we turned the corner near the back door I simply said:

"I'm sorry, love, I've just got to go back home and pray."

Not waiting for a reply, I began the short journey home as fast as I could while at the same time the battle continued inside my mind.

I went straight upstairs into the bedroom in our home and began seeking God for help in every conceivable way I could think of, in an attempt to get free. I thumbed through the Scriptures anxious for inspiration to pray. I called out to God for help to get rid of this foe within which seemed unshakable! It must have been a struggle lasting two hours, during which time I heard the demon suicide clearly whisper:

"Why don't you go and throw yourself in the Dearne? It'll soon be over!"

The River Dearne was a small distance away and I had a picture in my mind of a certain spot as the demon spoke. I fought on, mustering all the spiritual strength and opposition I could from God's word by repeating Scriptures rapidly as the battle intensified to take my mind. Then, suddenly, it occurred to me to begin speaking in tongues and fight the evil spirits with this unknown strategy demons are unable to understand and cope with. I had received this gift of speaking with other tongues at the Assemblies of God Conference a few months earlier.

At that time, having decided to attend the late night "receiving meeting" at the conference, I had said to Pam:

"I don't understand anything about speaking with other tongues, but I'm going along tonight because I'm eager for all that God has to give me."

Former Bible College Principal John Carter conducted the session wearing a mackintosh, and after a brief explanation told all of us to allow the river of living water of the Holy Spirit to flow out of

◆·◇·◆◇··◆◇··◆◇··◆◇··◆◇··◆◇··◆◇··◆◇··◆◇··◆◇··◆◇··◆◇··◆◇··◆

our mouths.

When he came to me all I could say was, "Hallelujah!"

He replied: "Never mind 'Hallelujah' right now, begin to speak with other tongues."

And then I did — it was as easy as that. A torrent of words I didn't understand flowed out of my mouth and heart and continued right up to, and beyond, the time I knocked on the chalet door. With my face aglow, Pam was as pleased as she could be, knowing that the Lord had met me.

What a provision from God it was going to prove! I began speaking very quietly in tongues, conscious all the time of the battle against the suicidal spirit still raging in my mind. It was only after 15 minutes or so when the strength of my voice increased that I was aware of the indwelling power of the Holy Spirit beginning to get the mastery. I got off my knees, walked the length and breadth of the bedroom speaking as loudly as I could. The joy of impending victory began to touch my life as I realised that my precious Jesus had moved in to fight the battle.

When I was assured that God had given me the upper hand and the satanic attack had retreated I began to praise God in tongues for giving the victory. The demon of suicide was not cast out that day, however, and reappeared in strength years later. God alone knew the sheer desperation of that day; mere words are unable to convey the internal struggle that ensued.

Thrilled with the joy of victory, I felt the need to tell someone what Jesus had accomplished, and ran to a Christian friend living in the next street, before rejoining my wife and daughter with the current crisis over.

For the next two and a half years I continued working at the colliery. During this time I played an active part at the local Pentecostal church in preaching and leading a weekly children's meeting, even though my struggle for inner freedom was still hindered by demonic forces. I failed an interview at the London City Mission purely because, so I believe, I must have left Duncan White, the interviewer, with the impression that I was carrying a personal problem conveyed in my brief, pointed answers and general demeanour.

In 1970, I made the unwise decision of giving up my job

because I was unable to cope with the work at the pit. Jobs which I had managed to keep on top of quite easily before now demanded more concentration, and proved immensely more tiring thinking about the doing than the actual performing. I sat at my desk in a state of tension over when the phone would ring.

My two bosses observed that it was taking me much longer to do jobs which I previously accomplished almost as soon as they appeared. Typing letters, filing and other office work which I skipped through with ease before, now required a determined effort to complete. I was even wrongly questioning receiving some work because of only being able to manage a small workload.

Filled with a tremendous fear that I would not catch up on the backlog on the last day at work, I stayed behind after everyone else had left. But before an hour had gone, I just had to get away from the office, leaving a lot of work outstanding. I didn't have another job to go to. The advice of the mechanical engineer, to at least stay on until I had, just didn't make sense in the midst of life being continually lived in turmoil and unrest.

The conflict abated after a while and I began working as a door-to-door salesman with Betterwear household products. After a few months of repeated frustration in this work, caused through the inability to make enough sales and customers not wanting items ordered, I resigned.

There followed a period of unemployment, and then our attention was drawn to an advertisement in the *Christian Herald* for a Christian bookshop manager at Chesterfield. I got the job on the night of the interview at our home and after a short season of training on the job before Christmas 1971, I took up the position in the new year.

We put our terrace house up for sale and after a long search found a semi-detached Victorian property suitable for our needs now that we had a son, Philip, born in April 1971, as well as our little daughter Alison.

But before the sale of the house went through, the director and trustees became aware of my mental problem. I had failed to carry out a simple request to display a number of books, and my inability to adequately explain why resulted in a visit by two trustees to Pam, who revealed my illness of schizophrenia. My whole mind and body

seemed locked up that day, producing an inability to function normally.

Realising that I might not be able to keep my job if I didn't remedy my behaviour and give satisfaction, I exerted my will against tremendous internal opposition. Eventually, I was given a loving reprieve by the trustees. Very soon after moving into our new home, I had invitations from the town's Pentecostal pastor, Albert Hibbert, and the senior elder of the church, to be the part-time pastor of a small Assemblies of God Church at Brimington, four miles outside the town. The work had started following the memorable visit of evangelist Stephen Jeffreys to Chesterfield in 1926, and was now struggling with a small congregation.

I readily accepted the invitation, but after about two months I realised I did not possess the personal resources for both commitments of running the shop and church. Though I preached regularly twice on a Sunday and in mid-week for the most part of nine months, I found the struggle too much and exhaustion was beginning to be a problem by the time I resigned.

With Pam and the children, I then started attending the well-established Assembly of God Church in Chesterfield and immediately had an open door to preach occasionally. A setback caused us some concern when, due to inadequate sales in the bookshop and the high operational costs, it was decided to close down at the end of Christmas 1973.

Left without a job, I decided to apply to the Post Office in Chesterfield for work as a postman. As a teenager, I had thoroughly enjoyed delivering newspapers, and thought the job would give no difficulty. How wrong I was proved to be, even in the first weeks of starting. The intense pressure I felt in the job was an opportunity for the demon of suicide to reappear.

The common practice was to put newcomers on a particular walk called Peveril, reasoning that if you "conquered" this one you could do the rest. The details of the delivery covered high rise flats, two housing estates as well as many private houses.

When the postman who had been training me was withdrawn, I was gripped with a daily fear that I would never be able to finish the walk in the allotted time. I was not physically fit, and unused to so much exercise. In addition, I had to cover two "walks" on the

second delivery by bicycle, which made me thoroughly exhausted by the time work was over.

The attack by the demon of suicide assisted by other demonic forces came early during the delivery round one morning as I was walking upstairs in the high-rise flats. I had encountered such a weight of heaviness and internal pressure persuading me to end my life that it was a miracle I kept working that day.

Instead of the attack lessening it increased as I walked the rest of the delivery. The problem a schizophrenic has is not being able to relate his problem no matter what he may be passing through, and I couldn't therefore tell Pam the horror that was upon me. The internal fighting went on for days until, through the persistent resistance of aggressive prayer and faith, the attack subsided.

For over two years and four months I somehow managed to survive in a job which meant going out of the house at 4.25 a.m. and into circumstances of work where there was pressure in the first hours of starting the shift. As a way of getting the opportunity of pulling back on needed rest I joined a "set" duty which included an afternoon shift once a month. I was only too pleased to help colleagues out when they wanted to change their "late turn" for my morning shift.

But the routine of work, even for me — at least with my mental condition — only provided a "dead end situation". When the opportunity came along to have my name go forward for work as a clerk on the post office counter I jumped at the chance to get out. It was a miracle I passed a basic aptitude test for the job, sat as it was at the end of the morning shift. I remember almost falling asleep over the paper. Apart from driving my will to stay awake and answer the questions, I would have dropped off!

I had been working for nearly two years in the new job as a counter clerk when in the early months of 1978 Pam discovered a lump in her breast. I remember the day she walked into the post office at Chesterfield and joined my queue of customers following her examination at the hospital.

I sensed in a way that all was not well as I kept my eye on her while my queue got shorter, and then face to face, with the bandit screen between us, she asked if I could get time to talk. I closed

down my position and obtained permission to bring her into the back of the building.

She unburdened herself by saying that an operation would be required, the initial news of which had come as a devastating shock.

On the day of the operation, Pam's breast was removed, as the lump was cancerous. I was invited into the ward sister's office to be told by a young house doctor that all the cancer had not been caught and that it would ultimately progress to her spine. I asked the inevitable question:

"What is her life expectancy?"

The doctor replied: "It's not possible to be exactly accurate, but depending on the rapidity of the spread of the cancer it could be as short as a year."

"Well, we're both born-again Christians," I replied, "so we'll make it a real matter of prayer."

I left the small office with this news not having really sunk in and returned to the bedside where Pam's parents and our two children were gathered. Somehow, with God's grace, I was enabled to conceal the emotion that was going on inside my heart and joined in the conversation.

On leaving the hospital and returning home, the impact of the news began almost to overwhelm me. I got on my scooter and thought of calling on my pastor, George Parrott, who lived about 300 yards away, but there was no one at the house. I then rode aimlessly around the outskirts of Chesterfield, crying inwardly and sobbing with strong emotion. On passing our Pentecostal church, I noticed Lois White, a farmer's wife and friend, taking her two sons to the young people's meeting, and I stopped to unburden myself of the news I had just received.

Sharing my load with her brought immense relief. My in-laws were staying at our home, and so far I had not disclosed to them the news of Pam's condition. Up early the next morning, I went to Somersall Park to seek a quiet spot to pray. I was due to work on the counter that morning, but the pressure of everything was too much. I phoned in to say that I would not be reporting for work.

My dear mother-in-law, who was always such a support just by her being there, then said to me: "Come on, Jim, what have they told you?"

I told her and Dad the news, which I was aware I ought to have given them the previous night but failed to do because of the disturbing impact it had had on my mind.

When our Church got to know about Pam's condition, I received an immense amount of help and support expressed by people coming to the home and doing practical things. It was very encouraging just having so many standing with us.

The desire to pray for Pam's healing became an issue that many took on their hearts and a special week of prayer was soon arranged. Between 30 and 40 people turned up nightly to pray, an indication of how much she was loved in the fellowship. Pastor Parrott said that the Church had never been so closely united in love on an issue of prayer concern. It was indeed a most moving time to be in those meetings.

I remember being challenged in my own spirit over the question of healing for Pam. Some years before at the colliery, I remember the day an assistant engineer broke the news to us in the office that his wife had cancer and only had a short time to live. I remarked to him that if that was my wife I would go home, shut my door and seek God until I knew whether He was going to heal or take her.

Those words now came resounding back. So I determined during the schools' half-term holiday in October 1978, when Pam and the children were visiting her mother, to seek an answer concerning the matter with prayer and fasting. I was working at the time behind the main post office counter in Chesterfield, but on returning home each night I would not put on any lights so as not to be disturbed by callers. With the gas fire on low, and sufficient light from a small torch to read my Bible as I prayed, I sought for an answer. I only drank liquids of warm water and Oxo. I remember hearing Pastor Parrott come to the door one evening, but I didn't break off.

Pam and the children were due home on the Friday. On

Thursday, the third and last night, I had been praying as usual, wanting to know if God was going to heal, when He spoke into my heart very quietly:

"All right, I've heard you; get something to eat."

I went straight into the kitchen and began putting some fish fingers on the grill. Then suddenly, I said: "Well Lord, what is the answer?" And the reply I received was that He was going to take her.

From that day onwards I viewed the matter as settled and had no conviction to pray for Pam's healing. Others were telling me that she was going to get better and that I had nothing to worry about. But I had no witness to confirm what they were saying. True enough she needed strength from the prayers of fellow Christians in order to continue living, but on the matter of prayer for healing I felt that God had revealed His will to me.

My mental condition made it more difficult for me to face up to this gigantic crisis in the way I should, and looking back I can only thank God that HE CARRIED ME when the load got intolerable and I reached breaking point over and over again.

Having such a mentally taxing job and caring for a wife and two children in such circumstances would have been enough to cope with for any normal person without having a disturbed mental condition thrown in. The fact of knowing that Pam had a terminal illness sapped all my bit of remaining strength. I was, however, aware of God giving more grace, but unaware really just how much He was holding me.

It was no surprise that just prior to 1980 I was admitted to the local mental hospital in Chesterfield absolutely drained and in such an advanced stage of fatigue. This time, though, I was admitted under a Section of the Mental Health Act after hitting the Consultant Psychiatrist in my home with the head of a hammer.

I was gripped by the delusion that he was evil and intended to do me harm. So strong were the delusions beckoning me on to finish him off with the blunt instrument concealed in my dressing-gown pocket; evil spirits assailing my mind, reinforcing the need to do this,

that I felt I just had to get on with it. It was a very rare occasion when their voices had the ascendancy over the voice of the Holy Spirit in my life, and seemed to triumph.

A group had gathered in the living-room with Pam and other friends from church including Pastor Parrott. I waited for the opportunity to hit the consultant as he stood in front of the gas fire with his back to me. I took hold of the hammer-head and struck him on the back of his head. The force of the blow was lessened in a remarkable and strange way as I brought my hand down, though the impact was sufficient to send him reeling and dropping into an armchair. There was no alternative but for him to "section" me for my own good and for the safety of others.

I again underwent electric shock treatment and received medication. The support of my local Pentecostal church was, as usual, both constant and encouraging. A common expression of their love and concern was to convey my wife and children to see me in hospital. The weight of my mental condition was increased by the guilt I felt at being visited by a devoted wife who herself needed my support in the grave crisis she was passing through.

Though the time spent in the hospital was of immense sadness and dejection of spirit, there was only one lifeline to God I knew how to grasp tightly with all my heart — that of holding on through faith centred on His word. Though my mind was in utter turmoil and besieged by the hordes of hell in their relentless pursuit to destroy my life, it was the power of the words of the Bible that kept up the tireless fight of resistance deep within my spirit.

There was not a bit of enjoyment in my life at this period — just the feeling of misery caused by a bondage which — if only I could have shouted it out — I was just longing for someone to break in the power of Jesus.

How revealing it was of the lack of discernment in the Church at that time, that there was no one around to offer help to effectively address the deep entrenchment of schizophrenia strangling my life. But how comforting to know that God knew all that I was passing

35

through in such hellish, prolonged suffering; and in His own time He was to engineer circumstances in my life to lead me out into perfect freedom through healing and deliverance.

There was not the discernment around in the early 1980s as much as ten years later, but I believe with all my heart that I could have entered into freedom had there been hearts intent on helping me through assailing heaven for answers! So sad, even today in some measure, that the Church of Christ, while empowered by his life-changing Holy Spirit, lacks the faith to "move" stubborn cases which cry out for deliverance in countless lives. But praise God for His ministry of healing and deliverance in those Christians who are breaking the power of satan themselves, or in agreement with others are loosening the strongholds in their lives.

I was able to join my wife and children in a "Family Night" during an evening service at our church shortly after being discharged from hospital. While my general condition was stabilised through regular injections, I soon began to deteriorate in health, however, as the pressures of work and caring for my wife increased through her cancer becoming more advanced.

Another distressing time soon followed in hospital with the usual build-up of medication which completely numbed by mind and killed all emotion.

As is frequently observed in schizophrenics, manifestations of delusions are quite common. But because of a discipline in my early Christian life to tune in to the voice of the Spirit of God, I was not the usual prey to hearing voices as many admit. The delusions in mind, however, concerned another type through being influenced by a religious spirit.

My preoccupation centred around being exceptionally special to God with revelations about things that nobody else had. How the religious spirit unknown to myself magnified pride in my life. These delusions became major strongholds which were later defeated and broken by the power of God following much prayer.

The death of Pam in August, 1981, occurred when all emotional strength was spent, my mental problem severely advanced and immense weariness assailed my spirit. God was, however, watching over us and was aware of how much we could take.

The funeral over, I had to try to get to grips with bringing up two special children who missed the Mum they loved and treasured. I now had to be both father and mother, though I was totally ill-equipped to fulfil this role. Feeling the immense loss of such a heaven-sent wife who had both loved and supported me for so long, and in a deeper way than I could appreciate, I seemed bereft of an understanding shoulder to cry on, never mind inspire a bit of hope into my life.

Looking back on how I was given strength to cope fills me with grateful praise to God. With my mind being assailed regularly, even at the time of bereavement, I was able to have the right attitude towards Pam's passing. Everything I went through was very different from someone grieving while enjoying normal health.

Some precious writings of Selwyn Hughes confirmed what I know God had already put in my heart, namely that the proper response to the death of a loved one should not be resentment, or rebellion, but rejoicing. Though overwhelmed with grief in the loss of Pam, I was able to see by faith that she was now eternally secure in heaven with Jesus — a fact of great comfort.

5

Crawling on my belly in the Principal's study

Life was by no means easy in the months that followed Pam's passing, as I began to appreciate more and more just how much she had loved and cared for me. How I had depended on her for support in facing life in so many ways over the 14 years of marriage.

I drove my will to keep turning up for work to fill my day in the writing room at the post office with duties which I could never claim to be over-taxing, only mundanely repetitive. If it had been otherwise, though, I doubt with my condition if I would have been able to cope.

There were jobs which always had to be done daily like the changing of franking machines and dealing with complaints from customers missing their items sent in the post. The most difficult task after lunch each day was counting the takings from one of the stores in Chesterfield. Thumbing through notes and counting coins used to take its toll on me, and I was never more pleased than when the job was finished. I would have avoided my turn of pushing the cash trolley back to the strong room given the chance.

Each day I just longed for home time. I had neither the relish nor the inclination for work at this time, and the moment I went through the gates in the sorting office yard announced my kind of exit to freedom, though on reaching home I slumped into a regular routine of passivity. Early in the evening my children would find me upstairs in bed withdrawn from the real world — and how guilty I felt inside.

Though the loneliness of life used to concern me, I made few overtures for friendship as I could not be bothered and the effort was too much. If ever I was in a low state, I would always find a spiritual uplift from an elderly Christian widow, Mrs Edna Buckley, who lived less than two hundred yards up Chatsworth Road. She had lost her husband shortly before I lost Pam, and I was helped by the wonderful way she found God's grace to take her through.

She was quick to invite myself and the children for Sunday lunch immediately after the funeral. It was a great encouragement to know that when I struck a bad patch she would light up hope within my spirit. Pam and I loved having fellowship with her, and we both dearly loved her husband Philip, too. He had often brought Pam and the children by car to see me in the psychiatric hospital.

I thought it was wonderful how God had his people on hand to support me whenever it was needed. In addition to Mrs Buckley, there were Graham and Joyce Dobson, friends we got to know at the Pentecostal church shortly after coming to Chesterfield. We both had young families and the children grew up together, visiting each other's homes.

Graham and I were both deacons in the church. He was a practical man, had built his own Mini-Clubman car, and was always on hand to do countless practical jobs at our house such as replacing worn-out guttering or mending the new central heating boiler when it leaked into the kitchen. We would pair up from time to time with our sons to see the ups and downs of third division Chesterfield Football Club at Saltergate.

I had read somewhere that the grieving process takes quite a while to pass through, and that I should not even begin to think about getting interested in somebody else until two years were over. In my own mind I knew that I was not ready for re-marrying, though I didn't realise it was because I was not free of schizophrenia.

I had to keep up the regular routine of receiving injections of modicate or depixol. There were signs of coping better at work and I was given greater responsibility, though I was aware that if my superiors knew of the internal struggle I was having they would have kept me away from more exacting duties.

Being one of the senior members of staff, I was appointed to try out the responsible job of taking charge of the main Head Office

39

counter when the regular overseer was on holiday. Fourteen clerks came under my control with the additional duties of looking after the main safe and receiving cash deposits from main stores in the town.

Despite the unhindered, daily routine of the job, I never liked the responsibility in the short space of time I worked on the duty. I found being in charge of the safe in the writing-room which distributed remittances to post offices throughout Chesterfield and district much easier to handle, though there were difficult balancing problems to handle occasionally.

I used to take the job home with me in my thoughts, and turn up sometimes an hour early in the morning to get on top of the work. Then, it happened! The build-up of pressure reached a peak, and I suddenly snapped, ending up in Walton psychiatric hospital again. This was to prove a time of utter devastation and demonic attack, the like of which I never want to pass through again (and never will by the grace of God).

The satanic attacks on my mind were relentless. Seeing my life at a low ebb, the powers of darkness moved in to harass and assail and were desirous of breaking my spirit. I imagined everybody was out to kill me. I even suspected fellow-patients of having evil intent towards me. Workmen outside carrying hammers were going to use them "to do me in", and nothing was more sure when I saw them looking at the drains below the flooring in the hospital corridor than that they were intending to drop me down into the hole.

The onslaughts created so much fear in me that I would not allow myself to go to sleep. I resisted the tablets in my system. It was a case of continuously fighting the hordes of hell who must have been fancying their chances of finishing me off. Without the strength of the Holy Spirit providing resistance within me I would have given in, but God prevented me from throwing in the towel.

Knowing how much we can take, God usually sends to our aid at such times His angel of comfort and help. Mine appeared quite often in the corridor in the form of our new minister, Pastor Ernest Anderson, whom I regarded as God's messenger visiting me in my prison house. He sometimes brought along his wife, Joan, and what a joy and relief it was seeing them looking for me in the hospital day room.

One evening I just had to escape. I couldn't stand it any longer.

I had to get to "the city of refuge", or to be more precise, to the Pentecostal church where the weekly prayer meeting was being held. With thoughts of everyone watching what I was doing, and feeling intense pressure on my mind, I managed to ring from the hospital for a taxi.

I paced up and down the foyer of the hospital, wondering all the time if I had been missed on the ward and someone was coming to take me back. After what seemed a long wait, the taxi finally arrived, dropped me off at church, and a great feeling of relief came when I saw Ernest and Joan and other friends there. I had reached a place of safety from those who I really thought were seeking to destroy my life. It was typical of Ernest, seeing my desperate condition, to invite me to stay at his home — an invitation I readily accepted.

The prayer meeting over, we approached the Manse to be greeted by a police car and two officers outside, patiently waiting there to take me back to hospital. Because I was under a Section Order at the hospital which decreed that I must be detained for my own safety and the safety of others, my debunking had caused the officer in charge of the ward to send out the police. It was with some reluctance and heartbreak that I was escorted back. My heart sank as I walked into the ward and prepared to get undressed for bed.

Eventually I was discharged and tried to pick up the threads of life again, but still I was not free, though in my heart of hearts I just longed to be. To my Pentecostal friends I was accepted as having these periodic occurrences of abnormality, though no one had any discernment as to the real struggle occupying my life. I needed someone with discernment, compassion and authority from God to draw alongside and begin leading me out into freedom.

The illness of schizophrenia was becoming more and more entrenched in my life, affecting mind, body and emotions. The psychotic disorder over the period of about 20 years had led to a deeper bondage through this greater entrenchment. Whether one believes the commonly held view that the illness has its roots in the womb, where normally well-ordered cells deep within the brain are thrown into disarray, thus causing a genetic defect, it cannot be denied that the condition gives opportunity to evil spirits to possess a life, and so deprive that person of enjoying normal freedom.

Christian schizophrenics desirous of enjoying the freedom purchased for them by Jesus Christ at Calvary literally know a constant war going on inside their lives. Real longings to be free of the evil nature of this condition provide ample evidence to outsiders and doctors (the patients themselves don't need convincing) of the strong prison house that holds them in bondage.

Though I returned to work part-time in the writing-room at the post office, on reaching home I just crashed out. Weekends were nearly always spent in bed, while I followed a kind of recluse existence as the schizophrenic condition prevented me ever having a quick satisfying forty winks, never mind knowing refreshing sleep any night. More and more a tremendous guilt attached itself to me, knowing that my children needed me, and I was too weary and tired to be by their side taking the lead during the important years of school life.

It was to prove such a delight in years to come, when healing and deliverance occurred in my life, to know again what it meant to have a good night's sleep. Knowing how much I had missed out for so long on quality sleep and rest underlined why I needed to regain so much emotionally and physically after the great day of healing.

These were indeed days of spiritual struggle in which I couldn't trace God but only trust, though my amount of faith was often very low. While there was an ongoing desire by evil forces to take me into further bondage, God was all the time watching over me and providing the power to pray. To appreciate now that all the hell I endured was known to my Saviour, who had full control of my life, gives me an unforgettable understanding of His faithfulness and love.

On a spring day in 1983, the onslaughts by the evil spirits took hold of my mind compelling me to believe a gigantic delusion that a devastating world event was going to happen at 10 o'clock that morning. I had been moving around at home since the early hours of the morning through having had a disturbed night. I felt the need to go and see Dr Skevington Wood, the then Principal, at Cliff College about eight miles away. So I hired a taxi and instructed the driver to get me there at double speed.

I was agitated walking down Cliff Lane near the College during the minutes before 10 o'clock as the delusion gripped my mind and sought to make everything real, as every schizophrenic knows. I marched down the corridor, then into the office of the Principal's secretary, saying that it was important to see him.

Dr Wood was standing behind his desk as I walked in. I didn't give him any time to talk, but immediately began to take over the proceedings by imparting the burning issue on my mind. He then sat on an easy chair without saying a word, presumably trying to make head or tail of what he was hearing. Then suddenly, I found myself on the floor slithering across the lush green pile of the carpet like a snake, repeating endless other delusions as the demons were obviously at work in my life.

It would have been obvious to anyone with knowledge of the demonic just what was happening. What a golden opportunity it could have proved to engage some of the students in deliverance ministry and take authority in the Name of Jesus over what was manifesting in my life! But as Dr Wood was to tell me later, he was not acquainted with such occurrences, and I ought to talk with his predecessor the Rev Howard Belben who had more knowledge than himself.

For one whole hour I dominated the conversation, and then Dr Wood interjected: "The students are about to take coffee in the common room. Shall we go down?"

Despite my intrusion on his time, and the disturbing behaviour that took place, he remained at peace throughout the whole encounter. He always seemed to have a sense of God about him. I always felt he had time for me and would never cut me short. Even later on when I rang him at the College on a Bank Holiday as he was preparing to move house, he sounded as if he had all the time in the world to talk to me. It was as though he was always allowing for interruptions in life and was kept poised under the control of the Holy Spirit.

Having carried on excited conversation with one or two students in the Common Room, I told Dr Wood I would be on my way to catch the bus from Baslow just over a mile away.

"Are you sure you can make it?" he asked.

I assured him everything would be fine and proceeded to walk from the Common Room down Cliff Lane to the main road.

I kept up attending church, though I dropped off going to

evening service now and again.   It was through a divorced friend attending our church that I was introduced to Christian Friendship Fellowship based in Doncaster — a kind of Christian dating agency for those wanting to meet up with Christians of the opposite sex for friendship, companionship or even marriage if that was the desire. It might be the solution for the tremendous loneliness and isolation in my life and seemed a good idea, though I knew I was not ready for marriage.   Members could also join regional groups and take part in social functions together.

I joined up by paying the annual fee of ten pounds, and in return received a quarterly digest of members living in various parts of the country who stated their personal details, interests, hobbies and what their interest was in meeting someone.   My introduction to the agency was at a dance held in Sheffield to celebrate the engagement of a couple who met through CFF, an event made more enjoyable by the attendance of groups from Nottingham and other areas.

It became something of a hobby with an absorbing interest to study the details of women who had joined. I was on the lookout for a fully committed Christian and was not prepared to consider eventual marriage to a divorcee. Seldom did I light on someone who stood out as a keen believer and follower of Jesus who had made it plain in the few lines of details shown.

On joining, my first contact and meeting was with a young Baptist widow from Mansfield whose husband had died of cancer. The benefit of sharing our experiences over the telephone gave mutual comfort, leading to my first meeting since joining. Though a second meeting never materialised between us, I thought it boded well for further contacts.

I was informed in the second group meeting at Rotherham, during conversation with two women in their mid-fifties, about false details of age being given on the male listings, and not all members of CFF were genuine Christians.

"One man I met had stated he was 10 years younger than he actually was. He certainly looked it, even old enough to be my father and admitted the deception when I asked him," one of the women said.

I eagerly awaited the arrival of the quarterly handouts of details of new members and would make fresh contacts by telephone, even in far-away places like Sussex. One part of my mind would say to me that it was pretty worthless making contact with someone living so distant in the hope of forging a relationship. But it seemed an interesting prospect on dark lonely winter nights to light the fire in the lounge and entertain the pleasing adventure of getting to know someone even in a remote kind of way. Actually, it was the only interest that brought a bit of sparkle to my life.

The arrival of a phone bill one quarter, for over three hundred pounds in the mid-eighties made me realise I was taking the hobby a little too far, and caused me to curtail those calls which I knew would never materialise into anything. I began to narrow the field to contacts in the Sheffield, Leicester and Manchester areas. I met women from these places, but it was not right to proceed in a relationship with them. Some obviously discerned that I was not completely free and this provided a reason for a swift end to contacts made, though my condition of schizophrenia was never known. I myself refused to admit that I could be labelled by that word, though I knew I had a real mental problem.

I often wondered if it was the right time to stop having my fortnightly injections. The longing to be free was often associated in my mind with ending all treatment, but I thought I ought not to make a rash decision. A psychiatrist had confused me by saying that it would not be necessary to keep having treatment throughout my lifetime. Perhaps I should chat to someone who would guide me. I proposed to do so when I went on a church trip to Lincoln to hear Rev Trevor Dearing.

Trevor, who was a former student of Cliff College like myself, had written a book called *God and Healing of the Mind*, detailing his personal testimony of how God had changed his life. Doctors described his condition when a teenager as "chronic depression," "hysteria" and a "severe anxiety state" and he also suffered from an intense depression, which shrouded his mind like a heavy, black curtain. God had wonderfully brought deliverance and healing to his life, which I was hoping He would do for me. If anyone could advise me about ending my treatment, he was the man.

I was inspired with hope as I heard Trevor preach and saw him at the close of the service ministering Divine healing and praying

45

with many people desiring personal help with their problems. It was not possible for me to approach him because of this involvement with others. As there was very little time before our bus left, I decided to talk to his wife, Anne, at the bookstall. I briefly explained my condition of needing injections following numerous visits to psychiatric hospitals. Her answer was brief but reassuring:

"Never come off your treatment until God tells you to."

And with that the internal struggle over the issue was settled.

Ever since Pam's loss, my children helped each other during the critical years of their studies. Again, I felt terribly guilty that I could not even muster either strength or support to get to most of the meetings for parents held by both schools. I often received stirring words to get me to "pull my socks up" from other quarters outside home but without the understanding of my condition.

I knew that my children were not ready for me to marry, as well as knowing it myself. I was to become engaged later on with a marriage date arranged, but it was not right to go ahead because the children were very unhappy about the wedding.

Work was shared between duties located in the writing-room next to the main sorting office and as a counter clerk. My patience and endurance with stamping pension books and being perched in one position all day long was beginning to fade. There must be a way out of this tiring kind of work, I thought. Month-end pressure, when car owners used to descend on us like vultures for road taxes was always a wearying time. And then there was the balancing. I used to be concerned about making a loss. Though I avoided making serious losses, this aspect gnawed at me and I longed to be free of it.

The only way out of counter work was to transfer to the Post Office Accountants General Department a hundred yards away in the town centre. But the thought of that routine work, which handled administration for all over the country, never attracted me to seek a change.

However, a chance came my way which I seized with both hands, though it involved exchanging my job only just over a mile away from home for a 26-mile round trip to Royal Mail's head office in Sheffield.

My reasoning in going centred on one main advantage — of

being in a normal kind of office atmosphere where I believed I would get stronger through not having the pressure of counter work. Some members in my family couldn't understand why I was moving away from a job on the doorstep, but it was a decision that was to result eventually in steering me towards healing and deliverance.

The move came at a time when the Post Office announced its Business Development plans, and I was given the option of putting in a request for a transfer. Travel subsistence would be paid for the first three years with a £1,900-plus payout all at once. In agreement with my children it was decided the time had come to have a new three-piece suite and a new carpet in the living-room. We soon directed the cash into those urgent and overdue improvements for our home.

Though working in Sheffield, I kept up the fortnightly visit to the hospital in the town centre of Chesterfield to receive my injections to keep me stable. I much preferred receiving my medication that way as it generally seemed to make me less tired. I could handle it far better than tablets.

For the first few weeks of the job in Sheffield I was a reserve, which meant filling in for someone on holiday. What a contrast to being at the beck and call of counter customers! The slackness of work and lack of urgency in the office routine soon enabled me to build up my strength. Eventually I was transferred to the Mails branch which dealt with all aspects of letter circulation, moving later on to the Datapost duty.

There were times, particularly in the winter, when I longed to be working nearer home, but the decision to move to Sheffield was going to prove an indispensable strategy in moving forward to become totally free, though it was still early days.

6

"Lord, I'm going no further than Birmingham."

Within a year, I was beginning to notice a vast improvement in my condition through working at Sheffield. Philip, now 16, was pressing me to take him on holiday to Majorca in the summer of 1987. I couldn't really afford it without taking out a £300 loan from Girobank, but I felt it was right for us to make the trip.

A few weeks before going, I decided to reduce the frequency of taking injections. It would be no use being on holiday and unable to join him in doing things. Injections sometimes made me feel tired and I didn't want to spoil the break for him by sleeping half the time.

I was pleasantly surprised that the staggering of the injections from every fortnight to three weeks, and then to a month, in the weeks leading up to going did not have an adverse effect. I was thrilled I had the energy to do things in his company. The excitement of driving him on a scooter around the island was a great experience, to say nothing of beating him at tennis!

Returning from the holiday feeling greatly strengthened, I decided to try again with Christian Friendship Fellowship. Pam had lovingly and wisely told me the night before she passed away that I ought to marry again for my sake and for the children's.

Perhaps now was the right time after six years to make another overture. In a short but pointed prayer, I told God one day about the decision, saying, "I'll try again Lord, but I'm going no further than Birmingham." God certainly heard my cry. For it was from Birmingham that He was going to provide help with a deliverance ministry on the pathway to freedom and healing.

I selected Tina's name from an old list which stated her interest in meeting someone with a "regular prayer life". She later told me that during her days of leading the dating agency's group in the Halesowen area of the West Midlands she had met many males who, though interested in a relationship, seemed to lack that requirement. Her few clearly stated lines were meant to ward off anyone less dedicated than that!

The details which appeared on the quarterly handout captured my attention. They said something to the effect: "Christina Winterburn, d.o.b. 1944, born-again Christian, interested in friendship, companionship, possibly marriage, likes cooking, travel, embroidery, Bible study. Requirements: someone with a regular prayer life."

She had relinquished the job of leader of the Halesowen group as she was being swamped by many "agony aunt" calls from women desperate to find someone. She had cancelled her membership altogether and was just another name among many that I had kept from previous years of handouts. She was surprised to receive a call from someone desiring a meeting.

This was pretty evident on the day I phoned. I caught her unprepared, but left brief personal details including my telephone number. She was to mislay these but prayed that if it was right to follow me up, God would bring my name back to mind, which He did. She eventually located me in the phone book, rang me and then we began corresponding.

In her second letter Tina wrote:

"I thought I would let you know more fully my connection with Christian Friendship Fellowship. I am still associated with CFF and receive the lists/news and letters, but for three or four years I haven't written to anyone on the lists. In the first few months when I joined, I did write about half a dozen letters but found the contacts not really committed to Christ.

"So then, I got involved in leading the local group here, but after three years of being at the helm I felt someone else should take over. I handed over the leadership in June this year [1987]. Originally, I joined because I felt isolated as a single person in my church. Also I felt quite lonely (for the first time in my life)

49

and felt the need to venture out of my orbit and make friends.

"I have made some lovely female friends in CFF and been blessed through their friendship. The few males I've met my age have been mainly divorcees with outstanding problems, so I haven't wanted to get involved in any way. Some felt quite hurt because I wouldn't go out with them, but I have always tried to be firm, straight and kind.

"To be honest, when you phoned me at first I felt quite defensive because of previous CFF contacts. I realised you were a definite committed Christian, though, and that kindled an interest, so that is the reason I phoned you back when I returned from holiday. Also, I sensed I had been somewhat abrupt to you when you first phoned me."

I discovered through corresponding that she was a former missionary with Operation Mobilisation in France and India and now worked as a practice nurse. It was a pleasant surprise to be told that her father, Maurice Winterburn, a retired Church of England vicar, had also attended Cliff College like myself. I purposely left out in my letters to her any mention of my mental condition or the numerous visits to psychiatric hospitals, thinking it would jeopardise chances of a lasting relationship.

After writing a few letters to each other, I invited Tina to come to Chesterfield for a day out. Our first meeting went well, starting with a lunch date in the town centre and followed by a visit to the picturesque grounds of Chatsworth House. It was a bright, late autumn day as we walked the spacious grounds, and I soon made up my mind that I liked Tina, and suggested a second date to which she agreed. She returned home to tell her father and stepmother that, to use her own words, she thought she might possibly have met the man she would marry.

It was during our second meeting at Tina's home in Halesowen, just eight miles south west of Birmingham, that she first began to suspect something was not right in my life, though it was too early to detect. Out walking the beautiful Clent Hills, I kept on referring to the many visions I had received over the years, which in reality were nothing but delusions.

To me these so-called visions were as true and as real as could

50

be but, of course, that's just one problem a schizophrenic has. These visions, I told her, were special, unique and important, but the way I spoke made me appear off-balance and a little strange.

We continued meeting at weekends for the next few weeks until she discovered my condition. She had phoned our home and was told by my daughter, Alison:

"Dad isn't in because he's gone to the doctor's for his injection."

"An injection for what?" asked Tina.

"For his nerves," was the reply.

When I later told Tina the injections were either modecate or depixol she put two and two together and discerned that I was schizophrenic, having shown some major symptoms.

The discovery that I had schizophrenia made Tina have immediate doubts about a lasting relationship. She had treated both Christian and non-Christian schizophrenics and knew there seemed to be no apparent cure. A Christian doctor at the practice where she worked had an interest in psychiatry and he strongly warned her not to get involved with me.

When Tina said to him: "If a person was married to someone with diabetes one could live with that fact," he replied: "There's a great deal of difference in being married to someone with diabetes and someone with schizophrenia. At least you can debate and communicate with a diabetic, but not so with a schizophrenic because his mind is illogical and unpredictable."

Tina was later to tell me: "He was really quite adamant with me not to get involved. He said it would lead to a lot of stress, about which of course he was absolutely right, until you were finally set free and restored."

His advice put lots of doubts into Tina's mind and caused her to decide, rather reluctantly in some ways, to start withdrawing from my life.

By early January 1988, three months after we first met, she had almost made up her mind "to let me down gently" and disappear from my life. Then something most significant happened in beginning a chain of events leading to a greater involvement with me.

I was off work for six weeks with laryngitis and bronchitis and had received an injection for my nerves. It produced a "high

condition" in me made worse by my having fallen in love with Tina. Into this maze of emotions, God spoke to me in my bedroom one night and gave me a real vision. His words were simply these: "Enough is enough," — a word directed to my long mental bondage, and I saw in the vision Tina dressed in a bridal gown with her father by her right side.

From that night I came off injections for my nerves (and haven't had cause to return to them). I began to pursue Tina, believing that I had the backing of heaven behind me. But word of my vision didn't impress her. Neither did the bouquet of flowers I sent by Interflora quoting a verse from the Bible about the bride and the bridegroom.

"He's high again, and this is just another vision," she told her dad and Esther.

Soon afterwards I went into the mental hospital for a rest on the advice of my doctor. I wrote a long love letter to Tina in readiness for her visit on a blustery winter's day and told her just how I felt. She sailed into the hospital wearing a long burgundy mackintosh, carrying tangerines in a string bag in one hand and a copy of *All Creatures Great and Small* in the other.

My first words were: "I want you to read what's in there, because it tells you all that I feel about you. I am deeply in love with you. You understand, don't you?"

While sympathetic with my mental condition, the romantic approach failed to impress, though in my heart of hearts I was as serious as I could be. She bumped into my Pastor, John Humphries, at the hospital and intimated she was going to walk out of my life and let me down gently.

Visiting my bedroom on the ward she saw lined up in the window a row of Christian books, mainly on prayer. She sought to inspire a bit of natural life into me by suggesting I read the book she had brought; but I made it clear that I had no time to read less important books.

I was helped and encouraged by a Christian doctor who advised me to take a new drug called sulperide. But I held on to the vision God had given me and was determined not to take any more drugs. I asserted myself and said to her:

"Whose life is it anyway? I'm all right. I don't want any more tablets."

During the short spell at the hospital, I never swallowed one tablet, although I gave the impression at the time when they were handed out by the nurse that I was swallowing them. I held the tablet at the back of my mouth with my tongue and dropped them down the toilet as soon as she had left the room.

In my feverish enthusiasm I kept ringing Tina from the hospital two or three times a day, causing some alarm by the number and persistency of the calls.

Her father Maurice and stepmother Esther were obviously concerned about her involvement with me. Their Christ-like compassion for me remained steadfast and they also prayed me through several bad patches. There was power being unleashed in my life in response to these prayers, and those from others in various parts of the country, as I received Christ's strength to fight the evil force entrenched in my life.

After discharge from hospital, I needed time off work for the laryngitis and bronchitis to heal. I bombarded Tina with regular despatches of "spiritual gems" from well-known Christian authors, which caused her to write in February, 1988:

"How many secretaries do you employ to send me so many letters?"

I was still head over heels about her, often asking myself why she didn't feel the same way about me. Receiving a letter always brought great encouragement to me, such as the one in February 1988, which said:

"I have been praying much for your continual healing. I believe the Lord has touched you, but sometimes the evidence of healing comes gradually. I was praying very much for you the other afternoon for an hour or so meditating on certain Scriptures. These are the verses that came alive as I was praying for a manifestation of God's healing touch in you:

1. Isaiah 26 verse 3: "You will keep in perfect peace him whose mind is steadfast, because he trusts in You."
2. Hebrews 7 verse 25: ... "Therefore He is able to save completely those who come to God through Him, because He always lives to intercede for them!"

3. Psalm 28 verse 7: "The Lord is my strength and my shield, my heart trusts in Him and I am helped."

4. Philippians 4 verse 7: "And the peace of God which transcends all understanding will guard your hearts and minds in Christ Jesus."

5. Psalm 22 verse 5: "They cried to You and were saved; in You they trusted and were not disappointed."

"As I have been praying for you, specific areas of your life have been major concerns of prayer, e.g. a restoring of a regular sleep pattern (10-11 p.m. - 6 am). I have been led to claim in the area of 'peace'. I want the Lord to continually immerse you in His peace.

"Also, I'm praying in these days you will learn to relax. You told me over the phone that you hadn't been able to really relax for years. So I'm praying that you will learn in these days. I feel you love the Lord 100 per cent and are fully committed to Him, but I sense you may have been spending time in feeding your spirit e.g. prayer/meditation but not enough time in relaxing following natural pursuits such as swimming, sports, hobbies, etc. Now, of course, our priority as Christians is to spend time with the Lord, but we are human and need to enjoy the natural pursuits of life to help keep us balanced. So I hope you don't mind me sharing that!

"The Lord really does love you James and wants you to show His life in the Post Office. You have done in the past, and I feel He will help you in the coming days when you get back and face the same people. I will be coming up on Wednesday and hope to have a long chat. I'm sure we have many things to talk about."

No sooner had I returned to work in Sheffield than a major financial crisis put me under considerable pressure. I had accrued a lot of debt from the use of several visa cards from Midland, NatWest, and Girobank. Strange to say I couldn't just put my finger on anything big that had caused me to keep using the plastic card, other than the Girobank loan and hefty telephone bills. I needed to secure a loan in order to clear the remaining balances on these cards.

The weight of owing the money hit me with particular force on top of everything else as I set off for Barclays Bank during my lunch hour to negotiate borrowing £2,000. The repayment amounts were about £55 a month for five years.

When the clerk arranging the details remarked, "That'll make it 1993 before it's paid. Seems a long way off, doesn't it?"

I replied: "It most certainly does."

The details completed, I knew the money would soon be available. This brought a tremendous relief as I walked back to the office from the city centre.

Having fallen in love with Tina brought its emotional stress as well. I felt frustrated that she didn't feel the same for me as I did for her. More progress would obviously have been made had I not had a psychotic illness, but how wise she was to keep me at arm's length at this time. A letter sent in mid-March evoked a reply that brought me up sharp.

She said:

"Thanks for your letter which arrived this morning. Yes, I do believe and am continually aware that you are in love with me. I am not offended at all by what you have written, but I'm a little mystified as to why you feel you need to repeat it from time to time. Do you feel my mind will be changed? The only thing that would change my mind would be if I had the 'go ahead' from the Lord. That has not come and if ever it was God's intention to bring us together then there would have to be definite direction from Him working through and revealing His will through circumstances.

"I am very fond of you James and the more I get to know you the more I like you. I am physically very attracted to you also, but I feel restrained by the Lord in committing myself to you, therefore I have to be disciplined and exercise self-control, which is one fruit of the Holy Spirit. I do believe (but I could be misguided on this point) that the Lord wants me to help you in certain spiritual areas. Generally, I believe it is unwise for a female to help a male through prayerful counselling, but somehow the Lord seems to have laid you on my heart. Also I definitely believe God has given me certain insights into you. I have said to the Lord, 'In many ways James is further on with

55

you Lord than I am, so why are you gently pushing me in prayerful concern for him?'

"There have been no messages/words of Scripture etc., to tell me to carry on searching for answers, but I have sensed intuitively that the Lord is just giving me certain insights into certain struggles and difficult experiences you've had in your life. I can honestly say, I've never had such insights in helping others in the past. When I've prayed about these insights all I can say is that I'm filled with peace, faith and even joy at times, but always peace and faith. So it must be of the Lord. Also when I've been battling in prayer I have felt quite tired, but as soon as I have moved on to a place of victory over your particular difficulties I have immediately felt a release of physical energy. Then I have felt I could move mountains.

"The contents of the last paragraph may sound strange or difficult for you to understand but please do not worry. The Lord is on your side and He is the God of Release and Restoration. There is a lot to talk about, James, and we are going to see more victories won."

Though the first part of the letter had brought me down to earth, so to speak, I became hopeful of things moving ahead between us. Somehow I seemed unable to grasp what Tina was trying to tell me, as I held on to the belief that our relationship was advancing well. I was totally unprepared, however, for the shock just around the corner on a day off in March, when she announced an end to everything.

7

"Today is our last meeting."

We had just driven into the car park and were walking towards the restaurant, when Tina dropped the bombshell that it was going to be our last meeting. It was news I was shocked to hear and refused to accept.

I replied: "This can't be," appearing half-stunned, and feeling that the bottom had dropped out of my little world.

Considering what she now knew about me, though, Tina had every reason to announce an end to our brief five-month courtship. When we first met in the autumn of 1987 she had no idea of my 23 years' history of schizophrenia; for if she had, there would have probably been no meeting from the outset.

Imparting the news of her intended finish brought more than a little sadness to her. I recalled that after our first meeting she liked me and even announced to her father and stepmother that she thought she had possibly met the man she would marry.

But to hear her now saying that today was the last meeting came as something I was not prepared to accept. It wasn't just that I was terribly lonely and needed a wife, but I was spurred on by the vision, in which I saw Tina in a bridal gown, to dig my heels in and not let her go. I was deeply in love with her, though in my heart of hearts I could not have handled what an early marriage would have meant.

So as we walked to the restaurant I remonstrated. "This can't be. I don't want today to be our last meeting," I said.

As we sat by the warm fire eating our meal, I wondered if it could really be our last time together.

Tina was somewhat shaken by my response. "I thought every

thing would be plain sailing without you putting up any resistance. At the end of the day I intended travelling home down the A38 never to return," she told me later. .

The vision of Tina in the bridal gown strengthened my determination not to let her go home that day without the promise of seeing her again.

Our meal over, we headed back to the car. Outside the restaurant I felt a little freer to state why this couldn't be our last meeting.

"I love you and I'm not willing that everything is going to end today," I told her, stressing that I needed her love, and the special kind of compassionate love she had for someone like me with a disturbed personality condition.

I must have stated my case with conviction, for at the end of the day when it was time for her to return home, we had agreed to meet up again soon. Before she left to return home, I shot up in her estimation by simply asking if I could pray with her, to which she readily agreed.

A mixture of emotions gripped my heart as I waved her off. I thanked God that I would be seeing her again, though we had agreed it would not be as often. I also knew a sinking feeling that without that promise, life would have been seriously difficult to cope with.

I sat in my home and reflected on the situation and how we first came to meet. Knowing that I had just avoided what for me was a crisis time, I breathed a sigh of relief. I still hoped that the 5ft 2in bright and bubbly nurse I had just waved off would indeed become my wife as the vision had shown.

Within a few days Tina wrote to me and said:

"I did not find it easy to communicate with you the things I did last Wednesday. I do not believe God is leading us together towards a permanent relationship and that is why I said what I did. Having said that I do honour, respect and like you, and I always will look upon you as a good friend. I do enjoy your company and I'm sure I'll see you again sometime. I'm praying for you James — I really am. The best thing you can do is to commit me continually to the Lord and to ask Him to bless and guide me. God has both our lives in His hands.

"I praise the Lord He has touched you and I look forward to hearing of the manifestation of His healing power in the months ahead. The Lord is powerful, the healer and sustainer of us His children. I will phone and contact you James. I will want to know how you are getting on and I believe God wants to show His glory through you in the coming months, so that your non-Christian friends particularly will be amazed.

"They will see His healing power manifested in you. In this healing process (and I personally believe a lot of God's healing is a process) there will be practical habits to be relearned such as a regular sleeping pattern. This is very important to establish in order to enjoy life. It was lovely to hear of you buying an azalea today — keep it up; they are beautiful plants aren't they?"

We met less frequently and the days apart were indeed difficult to manage. I had been through much worse circumstances during my long illness, and the grace of God was to undertake again. But the periods of separation proved so important in allowing Tina time to pray and ask God if there was really a way out of my condition. There were other matters, too, occupying her life, namely house-hunting. The year of 1988 was a time of booming house prices, particularly in the West Midlands and around East Anglia.

At the age of 44, Tina needed to pursue buying her own property. So she joined the many who were frantically securing houses before the prices soared high again. As a former Operation Mobilisation missionary worker in India and France, she planned to remain in work as a practice nurse in the West Midlands, a job she was well qualified in. But she needed space for herself and a place of her own.

Her father had settled in Halesowen after retiring from the Church of England ministry in 1979, and the property he occupied was his choice, bought by the Church Pension Board and rented from them. Esther, his wife, who was a retired nurse, owned a terrace house in Leeds which they still kept on as they made frequent visits up North to visit relatives on both sides.

On one occasion Tina was among over 20 prospective buyers escorted around a run-down terrace house for which she had made an

59

offer of £28,000. The whole party was a little surprised at the condition of the property, and one remarked to the company, "Well, if one of us doesn't get it, it'll certainly go in the Black Country Museum."

She wrote to me:

"The way house prices in the West Midlands are rocketing up is quite alarming, but I know the Lord will lead me at the right time to make the correct offer. Thank you for praying for me, especially regarding guidance about buying property. Over the last few days, the Lord has certainly brought me into a peaceful rest about it. The next couple of months will be quite pressurised for me with house hunting. I'm finding even now with my church commitments that by the time the weekend comes I feel drained. This week I'm out three nights but I know I'm doing the right thing."

We were both missing one another. Tina wrote in another letter:

"If I lived according to my feelings, I would see you every weekend, but circumstances seem to make that impossible at present. I will see you in July — what about the first weekend? We'll see nearer the time whether I come to your place or you come to mine. I'm sure in the future we'll see more of each other though. I have to confess I missed you last weekend.

"You're often in my thoughts and I pray you'll become stronger and stronger in mind as the months progress and that you will enjoy life much better than ever before."

The difficulty in keeping my job going amidst the inner turmoil and the comments to step up a gear in productivity became a constant struggle. In utter desperation and anguish of heart, I was more and more cast upon God in prayer and was aided to wage war against the indwelling spirits through the greater power of the Holy Spirit. God owned my life, and because of the power available to me through the death and resurrection of His son, Jesus Christ, He wasn't going to lose the fight. How faithful and mighty He was to prove in the next major battle!

For the space of four days I was really praying to keep alive, so intense was the struggle. The attacks culminated on the last night with such a tremendous assault on my life by the demons that I reached what I called "wits' end intensity". Finally, all I could do was to stay on my knees wrestling in deep anguish against this powerful evil force that was trying to overpower me. As I was being attacked in my mind, the stronger power of the Holy Spirit was strengthening me to fight the spirits inside my schizophrenic prison.

The final contest was fought on my knees into the early hours of the morning, though I was unaware of time during the battle. It must have been a few hours' struggle before I knew God had got the upper hand. Strange though it is to describe or picture, all the demons inside me, though not cast out, seemed stripped of their strength and were subdued within my life, if only for a time.

The physical and emotional toll was immense. I slumped into a chair and said:

"Lord, I just do not want to go through that ever again!"

God knew it would not be necessary. It seemed so significant a breakthrough that at the time I thought it was the full package to freedom. What the incident did was to impart such an important victory into my life, paving the way for the great day of healing and deliverance still nearly two years away.

By the end of June 1988, I had reached a place of utter helplessness and weakness. I had no more strength to fight. So hopeless did my situation seem that I thought the only way out would be to seek medical retirement; but the more I thought about that option the more guilt gripped me as I battled with the pressure of it being the coward's way out. But the whole idea seemed attractive. I had reached the point where I could drive myself no longer.

I apologised to my children for my lack of energy. I felt no one understood what was going on in my life and the only way out would be to throw in the towel. For years and years I had fought a hidden foe within my life. Contest after contest had worn me down. From my bed I said to Philip:

"I'm sorry, but I feel so lifeless and out of sorts."

He had seen me like that many times before, but on this day it was different.

In a moment of inspiration, I decided to get away for a break and

go to Scarborough for a few days, but the tremendous guilt I felt in even imparting this news to the children was hard to bear. I managed to muster enough energy the next day to pack a small case and set off for the train to Scarborough with a change at York.

The Yorkshire seaside town held many happy memories for me. Well over 20 years earlier at a time when my illness first broke, Pam arranged a brief holiday there in 1966 after I had come out of the Middlewood Sanatorium in Sheffield.

Walking out of Scarborough station in search of a hotel, my emotions filled up. Here I was on my own in a place which held such sweet memories that I just wept inwardly. A short way from the station I stumbled across a Christian bookshop where God was to minister to me very personally. Opening the door, I heard the popular hymn, "The Servant King" being played on an audio cassette. With my back turned to the counter, where a member of the staff was working, I cried inwardly as the words of the hymn came to mind: "And in the garden of tears my heavy load He chose to bear." I thought: "Lord, You know what I am passing through and You have great compassion towards me."

I moved to another part of the shop to look at some attractive posters and my heart leapt as I saw an attractive scene of a stream and flowers showing the words from Isaiah 42 verse 9: "See, the former things have taken place, and new things I declare; before they spring into being I announce them to you." A word in season indeed which inspired real hope into my depressed condition!

I stayed in a couple of hotels spending time resting and walking within a short radius overlooking the sea front. But I was holding on to God in prayer in spite of the mental tiredness and confusion. It was a break that brought a slight improvement in my condition, but by no means did I return home fully strengthened and free of the problem I had when I left home a few days earlier.

The day after returning home, a most important letter arrived from Tina expressing the view that she thought it was right not to physically see or meet each other for six months. She wrote:

"I feel very drawn to you James as you well know. The main thing that has always attracted me to you is your gracious, kind and loving spirit. Over the months that attraction has matured

and I have grown to love you.

"I would find it difficult at the moment being just a good friend to you. I feel, therefore, it would be the right thing to have a break for six months. I don't find this easy to tell you, and I certainly do not find it easy to accept; in fact I find it very hard. I've been thinking of you so much this couple of days. However, I feel before the Lord that this suggestion is right, but I miss you James and no doubt I'll miss you more. I do want you to feel free to telephone or write to me whenever you want to. You are really on my heart and I'll be praying much for you in the coming months.

"I really do trust that you'll have more fellowship with people in your church. Mixing with godly people does help us emotionally, mentally and spiritually. I think there must be many people in your church who love you Jamesie. I am praying that the Lord will refresh and invigorate you and pour more mental energy into you. Do keep in touch. I carry you in my heart and you're regularly on my mind. We must keep looking to Jesus. He is our hope."

Tina's decision to call for a six-month break was in itself the best thing that could have happened at the time. I needed the rest and break from seeing her because I was passing through a most difficult period. The effect of withdrawal symptoms through not having had an injection now for about six months exacted its toll on my whole system causing a reaction which made the need to pray harder more urgent.

I moved to the Datapost duty at the office where Sheffield Royal Mail was a subsidiary distribution centre, and the duty was quite demanding. I didn't realise it at the time but the pace of my work needed moving up a gear. Each and every day there was internal struggle going on in my life far more difficult than attending to office work. Although I had to be out of the house by seven every morning, I still believed that the change of location was proving to be a good one and I had no regrets.

I began to add fasting to prayer, and remember the day I walked into the toilets, vowing I would pray until freedom came. I adopted a daily routine of going into the toilets to pray both in the morning and

afternoon tea breaks and my lunch-hour, though the temptation not to pray was a daily battle. I used to determine before leaving my desk where I was going, so I set my face to head for one of the four sets of toilets and hide myself away with God. Even the pleasant smell of bacon and eggs coming from the canteen on the fourth floor didn't draw me! The devil kept ragging me by saying:

"Everyone knows where you go at break-time, and all of them in the office think you're a bit strange."

But the goal to keep my freedom and to increase it was the greater issue that remained on my heart and I rehearsed the journey in my mind each time. Once shut away in prayer, I thanked God for keeping me thus far and then went on to commit to Him the next stage of the working day.

On numerous occasions, the presence of the Holy Spirit drew very close during those prayer times, so much so that I could have stayed longer enjoying God. I was often reluctant to go back to my desk where I knew there would be an ongoing battle of endeavouring to hear the voice of the Holy Spirit in my spirit. As I performed my work, I closed my ears to all manner of conversation that I felt was unhelpful in my struggle. My love for God's word increased as it became a powerhouse in my spirit and affected my mind. Satan and the demons knew that the fight I was putting up was no half-hearted matter. I was determined to get free at all costs. God's word shone into my spirit and I "saw light in His light."

Boldness entered my spirit as I appropriated more and more the finished work of Christ for me on the Cross and declared the price that He had paid to set me free. When using the Bible as a weapon of prayer, I realised more and more what a mighty weapon it was for the pulling down of strongholds (2 Corinthians 10: 4). I didn't realise it fully at the time, but great advances were being made. Each prayer was having its effect, like a battering ram coming repeatedly against the gate of a castle and weakening it with each strike.

In addition to my increased praying there was the constant praying of others who were desirous of seeing me break into freedom. Tina was always aware of the need to keep me on her heart in prayer and she gave others specific requests to pray for. High on the list was that I might be able to see the complexity of my condition and that somehow God would break through and

"penetrate the bars of iron and the gates of brass encased around my mind." I didn't as yet have the revelation that I was schizophrenic. All I knew was the fact of being occupied in a battle; a mere name about my condition meant nothing to me, and I opposed anyone who labelled me "schizophrenic".

Tina told me how much Esther, her stepmother, used to pray for me, and her father, too. Not only in their own devotions but joining forces together when emergencies arose, such as the time when my favourite aunt was dying with cancer in early January, 1989. No doubt the effects of their praying helped me cope with what followed after an incident of jumping off the wrong Inter-City train in Sheffield Station.

As well as incurring the displeasure of the Rail Transport Police, I landed a bill of about £160 for delaying the train and damaging a door which crashed onto the wall inside the tunnel as the train pulled out. The emotional toll produced by that crisis, when added to everything else, required more strength. I was helped through regular praying by Tina's friends at Christ Church the Lye and Stambermill, near Stourbridge, who were always taking me to their hearts. Life-long friends up and down the country also took hold of the burden to see me free.

Tina thought we would both profit from a holiday in Scotland; but instead of it being a time of strengthening and refreshing, it proved nothing but an ordeal for her. Staying at a guest house run by two radiant Christian spinsters in Kinlochleven provided a happy atmosphere. But there were times when Tina saw parts of my difficult personality which convinced her more and more of the complexities of the illness and how vacillating were the mood swings it engenders.

On two occasions there were incidents that impressed the hopelessness of my condition on her. Driving into Glencoe one day with the cassette playing singer Keith Green, she observed that I was crying profusely without showing one ounce of emotion. It became worse for her when she asked me what was the matter and I couldn't explain. The words of the song had gripped my heart. Inside I felt so weary of all the problems in my life.

Knowing that Jesus understood brought great comfort, leading to a "quiet outburst" of tears. I was unable to explain anything to her,

which at the time proved most frustrating.

But a greater time of confusion and exasperation for Tina was on the day we parked the car by a lake. In the dialogue between us, she saw more than ever glimpses of the darkness of the schizophrenic mind with its patterns of illogical thinking processes and unstable decisions. That day decided her, in one sense, of how taxing it would be to get involved with me if ever marriage was on the cards. The holiday turned more into a strain rather than something she had hoped would be enjoyable. However, in spite of everything she was concerned for me.

In a letter received after returning home, Tina let me know just where she stood in our relationship:

"As I shared with you, I would wish to see greater mental strength before committing myself in a permanent relationship. So I'm praying about seeing evidence of normal mental strength becoming evident in the coming months. You are such a lovely man and I enjoy your company so much when you're relaxed, and I see Jesus in you, which of course is the most attractive feature in anyone.

"I have much more energy than you at present, and I love mixing with people, so that is another point to consider. I do realise you enjoy being with people when you are feeling fresh, but I love being with people even when I'm tired. Not always, of course, but I've often mixed with others at meetings, social events, even when I've felt very tired. In fact, at times I've been uplifted and strengthened being in the company of others when I have joined them feeling fatigued. So I find it difficult to want to be 'alone' on the whole, apart from times of necessity to do my chores at home or times of prayer, study etc.

"Be assured of my prayers in these days, Jamesie. There are good days ahead. Yes, you have felt much improved and I praise the Lord for that. However, I'm not satisfied yet, and so please put up with me seeing things differently to you at times. I do pray much."

Problems surrounding my slowness at work continued to disturb me, so much so, that I felt it needful to meet the Health Adviser and

put my case forward. Although it was a positive meeting, the letter which came out of it was unable to highlight the real reason for my performance at work, though I was given a sympathetic hearing. The letter sent to Personnel by the Adviser wrongly attributed my psychiatric symptoms to Pam's illness and subsequent death in 1981, adding:

> "Unfortunately, some symptoms were still in evidence last year following a withdrawal from drug therapy and which, he believes, affected his appraisal negatively.
>
> "Since that time, he has been symptom free and is now discharged from hospital and GP care. I am pleased to say his health is now fully restored and that the bereavement process appears complete. Mr Stacey is keen that you should know he is fully recovered as he now feels able to cope with further responsibility should that possibility arise."

Reading that letter later just impressed itself on me that the medical people at work had no idea what illness I really had.

At this time, Tina drew my attention to a forthcoming conference to be held at Brighton in February, 1990, called "The Battle Belongs to the Lord." She felt it held out hope for me because of the subjects to be dealt with which could be a problem to Christians, and she suggested I consider attending.

In the summer of 1989, Philip began a three year course at Reading University. Alison was already a student at Huddersfield Polytechnic and into her second year.

I earnestly believed that to attend the conference might give some hope, so I promised to book later. The devil was all out to prevent my attendance, though, and began scheming to prevent me. I lost my father in November and this was a big shock. Supporting my mother in the weeks and months that followed brought greater responsibility.

As time drew near to the conference, I doubted whether I ought to go, but Tina pressed and pressed me to make the effort, underlining that it might lead to the answer I was seeking.

I became more aware of the impact on the demons that daily prayer, and reading and living in the word of God were having.

67

Equipped by the power of daily reading the Bible and using it in spiritual warfare against the demons was most certainly challenging their home in my life. They were being stirred and felt under threat. It was during these days that God taught my heart the daily importance of standing fast in the faith, and how I should make it the issue of every day.

I began writing in a small hard-back notebook thoughts inspired by the Holy Spirit, and built up what I used to call "A Daily Familiariser". The important discipline every day was to pray and become strong through reading the Bible. I knew the importance of receiving instruction and strength from God's word in adding progress to progress in moving forward towards freedom.

I was determined that nothing would deter me from keeping up the fight to be free. What an encouragement to know that even though I didn't know how to pray as I ought in my predicament, the Holy Spirit knew how to teach me, as the Apostle Paul writes in the letter to the Roman Christians (Chapter 8). He was indeed continually "making intercession for me with groanings which could not be uttered."

It was amazing how the Holy Spirit was imparting spiritual truth and light to my mind day in and day out. I was getting stronger in what was a constant spiritual campaign against demonic forces. Moreover, hope was arising in my spirit that I could be set free, though it was impossible then to anticipate the depth of freedom until it actually came.

At one point I nearly told Tina to drop the idea of attending the conference because of the pressure of looking after my mother. But I finally gave in to her persistent canvassing and asked her to book me in. Her father and Esther expressed an interest in attending as well, and after a long search for accommodation ended in finding a flat for four in Saltdene, Brighton, the issue was settled.

8

"The Battle Belongs to the Lord" Conference

Little did I realise travelling down to Brighton for "The Battle Belongs to the Lord" conference in February, 1990, just how near I was to being set free. It was going to prove an important time, particularly for Tina in providing new teaching about deliverance and assuring her that my case was neither helpless nor hopeless.

About 3,000 people from various parts of Great Britain and other nations converged on the seaside resort to occupy the centre often used as the venue for the national conference of the Conservative Party. Being among so many Christians who were desirous of knowing more about healing and deliverance, was a tonic in itself.

Subjects listed in the programme such as Rebuilding the Shattered Life, Breaking Bondages, Liberty for the Captives (for those already Christians), How to Prepare a Person for Healing and Deliverance, suggested that this was going to be a different kind of conference, as indeed it proved to be.

The main speakers were evangelist Bill Subritzky, for many years a senior partner in a large law firm and governing director of one of New Zealand's largest home-building companies; Peter Horrobin of Ellel Ministries, and Graham Powell, engaged in evangelistic and pastoral ministry in New Zealand, Australia and Canada.

It was a conference I shall never forget, though I failed to absorb most of the teaching because of my condition. But God was ministering to me during the whole of the meetings, and advances

towards freedom were being established.

Sunday, 11th February, marked an unforgettable day for Nelson Mandela, the African National Congress leader, who was released from 26 years' confinement on Robben Island. Unable to venture out because of a gale hitting the resort, we watched his release on television with immense interest in our upstairs flat at Saltdene, just outside Brighton. Great anticipation was created before we saw him emerging as a free man.

On hearing of the length of his confinement, I thought, "That's about the length of time I've been in my mental prison." Seeing him obviously rejoicing that his long spell in prison was now over, a tremendous surge of emotion and excitement gripped my spirit. I was getting fortified in my struggle to move forward with greater determination to seize my freedom. I envied him in his breakthrough, though I myself only had to wait a matter of weeks to break an imprisonment far more serious and entrenched.

In the early stages of the Conference, it was made more than plain that Christians could be affected by demonic forces, even though they possessed genuine experiences of knowing Christ. Believing in Christ and receiving His new life at conversion did not necessarily mean that everything in the soul life had been dealt with too. I said a hearty Amen to all that.

Graham Powell made this point so clear in dynamic testimony. As he unfolded how from his earliest days the powers that gripped his mother influenced and gripped him, I was impressed how his story was very much like my own. His mother, just like my mother, was plagued by fear all her life. In his book, *Fear Free*, he writes: "She was so anxious, so full of worry, so swayed by a variety of fears. If only she had met Jesus as Deliverer, my childhood would have been so different. But can't we all say this? Rarely do parents, even Christian parents, understand the extent of the subversive activities of Satan. Because of our ignorance we offer no resistance, and evil spirits continue their works of destruction."

Hearing him describe the tremendous problems that came into his life and how great a struggle he faced in breaking their hold through the power of faith, drew a sympathetic response from me. I thought: "He's really been through it, just like me. But now he's free. Do it for me, Lord, too."

Despite the numerous mentions in the meetings of Christians being affected by demonic forces, it never really occurred to me that they were the problem in my life. Even when Bill Subritzky related how he came into the deliverance ministry through a demon entering his nine-year-old son and remaining for nine years, nothing spoke deeply enough into my life to suggest that my battle was with the spirits of darkness.

People interrupted the proceedings as demonic forces left their lives and I rejoiced with those who were being freed. During ministry time, a woman near to where I was sitting was being troubled by a spirit of hate towards her mother. I wanted to join the group gathered around her to add my contribution in leading her into freedom. I was new to commanding spirits to leave people and really didn't know what I was doing, but I could sense the woman was not in control of her life as her eyes seemed ablaze with another power which called out to her mother: "I hate you!"

In addition to meetings in the main Conference Centre, other workshops were held on freeing those affected by Sexual Abuse and How to Minister Evangelism. We never missed an opportunity to attend every session possible, though Tina was constantly aware how I looked detached during the meetings.

She was to tell me later: "I never thought anything was registering in you and wondered if the meetings themselves were providing any kind of help or breakthrough. You seemed to be in a world of your own, unable to pick up what was being said. I was a bit frustrated since you seemed to be immune to everything that was happening. Even in the worship time I noticed you were detached."

I agreed with her, but I do believe that since my inner ear was always striving to be hearing from God some light was penetrating, albeit in a small way. The problem a schizophrenic has is that his life in thought and action centres around himself in a most strange and too-absorbing way, unable to relate to normal life, never mind being able to grasp seeing himself as others see him.

Tina didn't receive much help on the subject of schizophrenia during the conference but received faith to believe that I could be freed of this psychotic condition. She was encouraged to hear how God dealt with a wide variety of strongholds in people.

"I believed that you had a demonic presence in you but didn't

recognise what it was," she said. "There can be in certain cases wrong attitudes and a number of wrong habits formed in a person because a demonic presence has ridden in. Through self-will a spirit of rebellion can come in as well."

The last meeting of the Conference over, I thought it would be a great idea to buy a copy of every cassette from each meeting. I wondered about ringing my home church, Zion Pentecostal in Chesterfield, to get permission to spend a bit of cash to buy them all, thinking how beneficial and helpful it would be to many in my church. But having second thoughts, I decided to use my own money and make the purchase. Tina bought a couple of videos, and together I thought we were armed with deliverance dynamite.

Convinced now more than ever that I could be set free, Tina began to increase the prayer assault against the demonic forces in my life by calling on the support of so many friends. As usual, she continued to see the importance of challenging me about wrong thought patterns and any wrong behaviour. She had done this in the early stages of our relationship, reading chunks out of *The Spiritual Man* by Watchman Nee concerning the mind, the will and the emotions and in particular on the problem of passivity affecting my life. She believed that real progress towards freedom could not be made unless I first realised the extent to which I had surrendered my life to evil spirits.

But such confrontation, needful and effective though it was to prove, brought head-on friction in our relationship in a meeting at my home after the conference.

Tina suggested to me: "Your problem, James, is that your mind is full of delusions."

It brought a classic response from me which revealed the schizophrenic mind. I strongly disagreed as I replied:

"My mind is not deluded. Do you want me to be untrue to myself?"

Tina replied: "No, I want you to be true to yourself. Your mind is muddled. The filter process is not working properly in you and the delusions operating in you are aggravating a muddled mind."

By this time, Tina had had enough as she blurted out: "I'm going home. I've had my fill!"

I switched from being on the defensive as she began to pack her

case, and followed her from the bathroom.

But she continued: "I've reached the limit of my help for you James, and there's nothing more I can do. I can't discuss things logically with you because you can't see things in a logical way. I will always be your friend, you can write to me or ring me and I will always try to help you, but I'm exhausted and have reached the end of things."

Tina was to tell me later: "I saw quite a sick mind and so I had to be careful what I said. You would often go off at a tangent, mentioning your visions and delusions and would take up a rebellious attitude to me. You were insisting that I accept you as you were, but I could not have contemplated marrying you in that condition, as life would have been too unbearable."

As Tina was all prepared to leave, the thought occurred to me that I might be losing her, so I suddenly changed my whole attitude. By the time she left for Halesowen, I secured the promise of a future meeting, though when she arrived home her father and Esther immediately sensed the struggle she had been encountering as she unburdened herself about what had gone on between us.

"James is unable to see his own condition and is not responding," she told them.

Later, she wrote:

"They could see I was shattered by my whole involvement with you. I had never before encountered such exhaustion in a relationship. Leading a team of workers in India which brought its problems never saw me anything like this. The weariness I was feeling was that I was challenging demonic strongholds in your life which kept sapping my energy. It was at this stage that Dad and Esther advised me to keep my distance from you if only for the sake of my own health."

It was during another visit to my home soon afterwards that the same problem of needing deliverance reared its head.

"I need to take you round to Jill's to get some help to pray this demonic force out of you," Tina said.

Jill Stone was a member of the Pentecostal church in Chesterfield and a personal friend.

I replied: "If there is something there as you say, then let's go round to her house right now and get it out. I'm willing."

I was giving her a challenge through agreeing with her, rather than offering my cooperation, as was seen when we arrived at Jill's house.

Sitting in a chair, I said to both of them: "Okay, if there's something there, get it out. I'm more than willing to see the back of this problem which you say I have."

I stayed there wanting them to start work, but by no means giving wholehearted cooperation.

"He's not with us in this," said Tina to Jill. "He's wanting us to do the work of calling out this demon but at the same time he's denying its presence in his life."

How important it was for me to receive more light and truth by the Spirit of God to reveal my true condition and deception. They couldn't continue because of my unbelief. As the weeks moved into Spring and beyond, a great offensive of prayer continued from many intercessors with the specific targeting of the need for me to see my own condition — a revelation that was soon to dawn on my darkened mind.

9

Delivered and healed within minutes

Although I was unaware of it at the time, the final battle against the powers of darkness in my life had begun. Their desire to destroy me after 26 years of real occupation was now being certainly threatened. I began to feel a nagging pain around my right knee, so excruciating at times that I could barely walk. I discerned that the demons were located there.

It may seem strange that the cause of a mental bondage should be found so far away in the lower part of my body, but sure evidence to me of how long they had been in my life and how deeply they were entrenched. The story of the crippled woman healed on the Sabbath day as recorded in Luke, Chapter 13 confirms the fact that evil spirits can be responsible for bodily pain.

The pain was present one night when I visited my father's memorial in the village cemetery in South Anston. Immediately I stepped into the graveyard, it was felt pain with such power as to resemble an ambulance siren being switched on.

Tina kept up the fight to free me by seeking help from her team of intercessors. She also contacted Bruce Hunt, involved in Christian counselling, who lived in Worksop.

He was most helpful in discerning my problem and told her that my mind was like a dungeon with many compartments, each having its own shutter.

"The double vision signifies the real and unreal, where there is an inability to work out and understand day to day living. Some of these compartments are shuttered from the bottom, and it's light against darkness and this is causing confusion," said Bruce.

A great step forward in destroying the powers of darkness encircling my mind came during a weekend of prayer and fasting in late March 1990, which Tina spent with Joan Clark. Over two days, they not only made great advances in securing answers for others, but God dealt with issues in their own lives resulting in bondages being broken.

She added that in the prayer time for me they took hold of the promise in Isaiah 45, verse 2b in which they asked God to "break down gates of bronze and cut through bars of iron" around my mind. Hope of securing a breakthrough in my life gripped them both, with Tina observing:

"When these are removed, then the Lord can show you step by step (and it will take some time) those areas where you will need deliverance. Present this before the Lord. Be assured of mine and Joan's prayers. I want to assure you of my esteem and love and I will continue to stand in prayer for you. In fact I have committed myself to continue praying for you and I will be in contact; whatever you think or feel be assured that I'm carrying you frequently in prayer. You are lovely and one day you will fully flower, I believe. So do please keep in contact. How else can I pray intelligently for you? I don't know what God's ultimate plan is for us. The Lord knows. Praise Him."

The extent to which more light was soon received from this prayer time, I believe, can be judged from my desire to write to the director of a ministry centre. On 9th April, 1990, I asked "for prayerful consideration to be given as an urgent case for personal ministry in healing, counselling and deliverance." Tina had also written to him detailing my problems.

The letter, covering four pages of A4, took so much time and effort to write that I set aside a day's annual leave from work to complete it. I thanked the director for the privilege of being at the Brighton Conference, and for the teaching and ministry received. I detailed the dealings of God with me since conversion at the age of fourteen, and stressed I knew I was not free. I desired a full release of freedom into my life.

Looking over my letter later, I realised that it contained one mistake. When God spoke to me in my bedroom in 1988 and said, "Enough is enough," it was not a time of receiving healing and deliverance. But it was the time I felt guided to discontinue the medication, curtail spare-time journalism and working as a church deacon in order to make prayer my first priority. It was a promise of freedom to come. I stated in the letter the importance of the breakthrough which followed prayer-battling against satanic powers over four days.

I wrote:

"I still feel (for want of a better word) a restriction on my freedom. Though the Lord has returned normalcy in many areas, I feel a lack of energy because there is a band around my mind. It does not prevent me from being productive or living and enjoying God, but it is 'a continuing infirmity.' I have goals to achieve for the Lord and I want this persistent thing out of the way. I feel that counselling and prayer and a word from the Lord will set me free and I shall be seen to be free as well as knowing it myself.

"I may have left important things out but briefly that is my reason for writing. The need to break free is so important to myself that I am willing to come up at a moment's notice. The return to complete health in the mental realm is the only factor hindering Tina from committing herself in marriage, though our relationship has always been directed to the will of God. I eagerly look forward to your reply."

The director soon wrote back to say that he would be able to fit me in for ministry towards the end of May. My hopes were raised on receiving his letter, though by the time I was to make the visit God had worked for me in response to so much praying and calling out to Him by imparting deliverance and healing — both within a matter of minutes.

A week before deliverance and healing took place, I received a letter of encouragement from Tina while on what I called "the last lap of a long struggle."

"Although you're feeling tired and even bombarded in your mind at present, in a way it's a good sign. The devil knows you

are onto something great. However, it's not God's will for you to become sapped of energy and worn out even before going to Ellel. So we have to defeat satan's tactics and strategy in trying to wear you out in order to stop you receiving ministry.

"Well James, you are on the winning side. Satan is a defeated foe and he has no right to harass you like this. During these last few days, I've felt quite oppressed and worn out but tonight I feel much better. I'm waging war and taking authority over the powers of darkness trying to destroy you. Do ring me anytime if you want to talk, to fill me in with what you are facing. OK? I know you have to watch the phone bill.

"Don't fast and pray on your own at present. Please don't, no matter how tempted you are to do that. Of course, there is a time to fast and pray but not for you at the moment. If you feel an urgency or desperation to spend excessive time in prayer then just PRAISE, PRAISE, PRAISE, PRAISE (exerting your will in PRAISE) and you will find the agitation or whatever will pass. The devil hates PRAISE.

"Do enjoy life during your lunch times — go for a walk in the park, or eat a delicious meal or play dominoes!! Do something you enjoy related to life. Even if you don't feel like doing something related to life, nevertheless do it. Don't let the devil lead you up any alleys, don't let him, resist him particularly through PRAISING God. I think some bars will be broken through PERSISTENT PRAISE. Don't let your feelings dictate to you at present what you should do. Exert your will. Here ends my sermon. If you can manage to write down each day a little of what you're experiencing, this will help the folks at Ellel Grange to help you."

The memorable day when I was set free was on a bright and sunny May Day Bank Holiday in 1990, the extra public bank holiday for workers to enjoy, but for me a day of joyous freedom through deliverance and healing. It was a day to be outdoors, so Tina and I headed for the Clent Hills, our favourite spot for a walk and chat.

During a leisurely stroll, Tina pointed out that my problem was one of schizophrenia. She said it in a matter-of-fact way, but no sooner had she spoken than the Holy Spirit said to me: "That's right.

That's what it is." I found myself totally agreeing with her for the very first time.

It was as though light and truth from the Holy Spirit dawned on my mind and I could see myself as I really was. No more disagreement or opposition from me, but a simple acceptance of what she had said. Revelation had at long last penetrated my mind.

Arriving back at her home, I was moved to ask if we could pray together. It proved a mighty time of aggressive intercession during which the Lord moved into our praying and carried me heavenward with powerful pleadings. I told God I was so angry with the enemy of my life for having messed it up all these many years. It was earnest petitioning coupled with a desperate cry for help, to me so urgent and real that I told Tina in an aside to be quiet because I was really talking with God and getting through, and it was important to unburden my heart and share my need.

I came out of that prayer more powerful than when I went into it, but I also received an assurance from the Holy Spirit that the evil power was going to be cast out and by the end of the day I would be free.

I could see that Tina was looking tired, as she often had been in her loving, devoted help to me for so long. The thought of having more prayer was dropped and I decided it was time to leave for home at Chesterfield.

We kissed and said cheerio at New Street Station, Birmingham. I was itching to get my teeth into a book called *Pigs in the Parlour*. I read of how evil spirits can, through lack of watchfulness or dabbling in the occult, be allowed to walk into our lives like pigs coming into the best lounge in our homes and squatting down in all their filth without being moved on. I spent the time before boarding the train praying in the toilet, asking God for a quiet spot on the journey so that I could read undisturbed.

I found a single seat right up front in the first carriage next to the engine. As I read first of all the chapter on schizophrenia, and then two more, faith and confidence began to rise in my heart. I really believed that God was not only able to rid me of this demonic presence but that He was going to show me how to do it single-handed.

On reaching home, a joyous anticipation of being set free

gripped my life. The fact that I had never before cast out evil spirits from my own life or anyone else's didn't seem to matter. I turned the whole business over to God and said: "Lord, you'll have to help me because getting demons out is all new to me."

The way forward came when God replied in an instant. "Blast them out," was the inspiration that flashed across my mind.

The Lord had given His directions on how to proceed, so I turned the settee into the bay window to give me privacy. Because satan and demons loathe intensely hearing God being praised and worshipped, it seemed good to the Holy Spirit and to me to declare in praise who was really on the throne of my life and who had the right to own all my life.

Addressing the evil presence in my life, I said: "I'll blast you out!"

So, using a cassette of praise choruses put together at my church, Zion Assembly of God, I sat on the settee with my right leg resting on an upright chair minus my sock and shoe. I played triumphant praise as loudly as possible from the recorder into the area around my right knee where the feeling of cramp was still present. On the train journey home the nagging power it always produced seemed muffled during the reading of the book.

When the 20 minute tape reached the chorus, "Jesus at Your Name we bow the knee", I thought it had particular significance to my praying. So I leaned over and addressed the demon in my right leg, saying: "Do you hear that, you demon of schizophrenia, bow the knee to Jesus!"

I then sat back waiting on the Lord until the rest of the tape ran out. I then turned the cassette off and with the Lord helping me, I challenged the demon's legal right to be in my life. I pleaded the blood of Christ and asserted the Lordship of Christ over my life, telling the demons that they had no legal right to be occupying my life because Jesus Christ of Nazareth had died for me. I declared boldly that they had been pigs in the parlour of my life for far too long and now had to go. I commanded the demon of schizophrenia to leave my life and go to the dry and waterless place, and THEN IT HAPPENED.

Glory to Jesus! There were two movements across the middle of my right leg followed by a third which was distinct from the other two, all going down my leg and out through my bare foot, providing a sensation of release. I knew without doubt that the evil forces had left my life. I believe the three movements represented a "nest of spirits" being exorcised, and were demons of schizophrenia, religious spirit and suicide.

I almost hit the ceiling with joy as I realised that God had won a deliverance in my life. Then I thought to ring Tina to tell her the good news. Walking to the phone in the corner of the room, the Holy Spirit checked me and I sat down on the settee. Placing my hands in three places over my head, I prayed: "Lord, believing that You have enabled me to cast out those demons in my life, You heal what has been knotted up in my mind for all these years."

As I was still speaking, God unleashed laser-type healing power right through the centre of my head. It was just like the promise in Isaiah 65:24 "Before they call I will answer; while they are still speaking I will hear".

On this particular day, He responded with greased-lightning speed. I didn't feel the impact of God's healing power so much at the sides of my head. The "rays" of power cut through the centre and I felt in a split-moment of time, power infusing the top of my head down to my forehead and right through to the base of my neck. It was God hitting the bull's eye in the area where I needed His healing power.

I heard in years to come an explanation of the dramatic events that changed my life that evening. In a tape called "The Substance of Prayer" on the subject of unleashing the power of prayer, Dutch Sheets of Colorado Springs mentions that for some prayers to be answered there needs to be a sufficient amount of power released "to get the job done". The more difficult situation calls for persistent prayer and the accumulation of those prayers, he says. God sometimes answers certain prayers immediately, but others need "more prayers from the saints of God" to fill up the golden bowls of incense out of which God sends the answer.

At a given moment, says Sheets, when the censer has been filled with enough prayers, God tells the angel to hurl the fire of the healing power of God to earth, so providing the answer required. (Revelation 8 verses 3 to 8.) The moment of breakthrough for me came that afternoon in prayer when God came into the praying and

81

the censer reached its fullness imparting the assurance of freedom. But the sending of the fire to heal my mind followed the deliverance from evil spirits.

Knowing I was now both delivered and healed, I raced to the phone to tell Tina the good news. Though she was tired, she fully entered into my rejoicing.

"Well, how did it happen?" she asked.

I then filled her in with the details.

"It's just wonderful. I'm so thrilled for you, James. God has answered our prayers at last. Blessed be His Name."

I was disappointed that Tina was not with me to see the immediate effect of healing on my face, now aglow and full of joy. The band of tightness around my mind was no longer there. Instead of my face being under the influence of a mind paralysed through deep entrenchment by evil spirits, it was bursting with joy because of the inner release. I said to Tina:

"I can't wait to get down to see you on Saturday. You will be meeting a new man. I tell you I look different."

I went to work the next morning in Sheffield feeling so very different, like a man having walked out of a prison house with his chains left inside the cell. The inner joy and strength enabled me to get on with my work a lot easier. There was no fear upon my life, because God had broken it in every form. I knew there was now power in my life through the fresh realisation of Jesus dying for me. The authority I possessed in Him caused me to walk ten feet high.

My longing to travel down to Halesowen to see Tina was with me throughout the whole working week. Every night I was on the phone to tell her how I was getting on:

"It's just wonderful. On getting home from work I don't feel tired. There's no need to go upstairs to rest or sleep like before. The healing has brought fresh strength into my life, and I'm living a new life."

The effects and benefits of deliverance and healing were both immediate and immense. Not only was my mind set free, but also my locked-up emotions and the straitjacket around my body dropped off. I felt no restrictions to begin such things like gardening, where the thought of doing the work before was actually more tiring than the work itself. I no longer needed to employ someone to dig over

my garden, such a small area that it had become something of a joke with one or two friends that I needed to engage someone to do the work for me. But in the past, digging had proved a problem to me as I lacked the physical strength. It was far easier for me to ask a gardener to come and do the work while I wrote articles for the *New Life* newspaper and paid him for his time and effort from the earnings received.

Wonder of wonders, I actually became interested in DIY, and my productivity increased plus the zest for living. The enjoyment of natural life, of which I had been deprived for so long because of my condition, returned. The delusion concerning legitimate pleasures left. I felt able to sit out in the sun without a hat on and really enjoy the heat on my head, as I now did in my lunch break on the lawn near the bus shelter in Pond Street, Sheffield, praising God and speaking in tongues.

The deliverance and freedom that Jesus had brought into my life was visible to all. My children saw a marked difference and got their real father back. Colleagues in the office observed a brighter countenance replacing a heaviness and tiredness around my eyes. It was a freedom and freshness hitherto not seen. Christian friends, too, noticed what God had done, though many didn't have the interest to ask how I had become set free, possibly because of a lack of understanding about the demonic influence on my life.

So eager was I to see Tina on the first Saturday morning that I made it down to the Chesterfield railway station and caught the first train. Waiting for the Birmingham connection at Derby station, I went into a photo-booth at 06.30 to take four quick snaps as joyful evidence to me, and others, of the great difference in my face that healing had produced.

Meeting Tina at her home, I wrapped her in my arms and was bubbling over with what God had done in my life.

"You certainly look so different. I can see that something has happened right away, because your eyes seem full of light, not like before," she said.

Our being together from now on proved so much more relaxing, and we enjoyed "bathing" in the new life that God had brought me into. I wondered at one stage whether or not I should still go ahead and attend the ministry centre for counselling and healing

consultation, now that I had been delivered, but I decided to keep the appointment, though not knowing what to expect.

By the time a few weeks had elapsed before going, I realised a little that there had been a 26-year gap in my life in which I had not developed naturally.

There were not only areas in my life to regain which demonic forces had taken to themselves, but I had to reorientate myself into life again. I later discovered this was going to take quite a long time. I came to realise that although the demons had left, the thought-patterns they had established in my life needed totally breaking. So I continued praying, waiting on God, meditating, doing everything I had done prior to being set free in order to strengthen my life.

I still continued getting out of bed at 5 a.m., even the first morning after arriving at the ministry centre. I walked downstairs into the main entrance to get a cup of coffee, and then questioned myself: "Why are you up so early?"

I realised it was now time to take things more easily and enjoy my new freedom. So I went back to bed to enjoy more rest and the added delight that at eight o'clock the sun began shining on my face through the already opened window. It was a time of peace and wonderful relaxation.

The time of counselling over two days proved both helpful and interesting as the two counsellors sought to lead me into greater freedom. Although they accepted my testimony of healing and deliverance, they were aware from the contents of my letter how strong the religious spirit had been. I cooperated fully with them in conversation and prayer, knowing of their keenness to help me.

During the next eight months, I gradually began to get stronger and stronger. Now I was free, I began pressing Tina on the question of getting engaged, but time and time again she was not being hurried.

"I'm aware that the Lord has done something wonderful in setting you free, but please give me a little more time before we decide to go ahead," she said.

When I was absent from her, Tina was doing a lot of praying and seeking the mind of the Lord whether to commit herself in marriage. I was anxious for us to get engaged and name the big day,

but in a way I was pleased she took things less hurriedly, as it gave me more time to start the long steady process of restoration and recuperation.

She herself needed space and was determined to avoid pressurised circumstances after locating discomfort in her abdomen and diaphragm area. Being involved with me emotionally and acting as deliverance minister rolled into one had taken an immense toll. I was in full agreement with her decision that until she sorted herself out, trips up to Chesterfield would be less frequent.

However, they say everything comes to him who waits. It certainly did for me in the early months of 1991 when it seemed that the vision of Tina in a bridal gown was moving to fulfilment, as we decided to announce our engagement in April. In my heart of hearts I always knew it wouldn't be too long in coming.

10

The Wedding Day spills over with rejoicing

An important lesson the Holy Spirit was constantly teaching me was to keep my freedom intact. The discipline of the spiritual life of prayer, reading God's word, and waiting on God were necessary to fulfil. I knew instinctively that if I was not only to maintain my freedom but enlarge it, I needed to do what the Bible calls "stand fast in the liberty" which Christ had now brought into my life.

I continued the discipline of early morning prayer in order to enjoy the wonderful benefits through meeting and finding God in the early hours of the day. Jesus himself proved it.

In the past, I had found it needful to throw back the sheets to pray in the heat of the battle. Now there was a greater joy and release in rising to pray following deliverance and healing.

I took the matter extremely seriously that I was definitely not going to lose my freedom. In no way would I allow satan and demonic forces to invade my life again. I heeded the warning given by Jesus in Matthew's gospel, that once having been set free it was important to keep free or else the enemy could return bringing with him demons "seven times worse" than the ones who had departed.

So at every opportunity when travelling to work on the bus or train I would pray, open up my little Christian workers' personal testament and meditate on the word of God. I had always been one for writing down inspirational thoughts for use in sermons, but now I "banked" them in a small hardback book and would categorise everything under headings. The issue of standing fast became the issue of daily living. I was determined that the only thing that mattered day in and day out was to both start the day and finish it

with God, keeping faith intact.

This had always been the emphasis during the days of struggling into freedom. I remember saying to Dr Skevington Wood that the Lord was showing me one important lesson on which everything else depended, namely that of knowing I was consciously standing fast in the liberty which Christ had imparted to me. He replied:

"You've certainly got it right. Everything stems from that."

I assembled all the thoughts God was giving me under about 15 or more section headings on the secret of Christian living that standing fast in the freedom of Christ imparted. There was an overlap in many sections, but I knew that here were the answers to being filled with the Spirit; living in the word of God, and the ability to maintain an effectual prayer life, as well as shatter the kingdom of darkness. Issues of loving God and keeping the unity of the spirit among fellow believers, I also found among the benefits of standing fast.

I mistakenly thought, though, that this discovery that God had shone into my heart must be known by every Christian. I soon discerned that this was not the case. It was such an important lesson God had revealed, indeed what I would call one of His secrets, that I was so sure every Christian who professed to be going on with God knew it too.

In mixing with Christians, I had the impression that there was a longing in their lives to know God more deeply and enter into the rest promised in the Bible. I concluded that God's best for a believer comes through "falling into the ground and dying to self", and then being really filled with the Holy Spirit, during which the secret of standing fast is imparted.

Throughout the remaining months of 1990 I pursued relentlessly this need to stand fast and keep my freedom. I was inspired by God's promise to Joshua in the early days of commissioning him as Moses' successor. If I meditated on God's word "day and night and allowed the law of God not to depart out of my mouth", I too would become strong and have good success.

I realised how such meditation had been important in preserving my life and keeping satanic forces at bay. One day I listened to a programme on my walkman in the lunch hour and heard a professional woman who had received electric shock treatment say

that after-effects had destroyed her memory. She wanted to write about her experiences but found that the treatment had both shattered her memory and totally destroyed all recollection of the past.

I rejoiced in my spirit over the mightiness of God's power to keep my mind functioning well despite everything I had gone through. To be delivered out of an insane prison house with my mind and spirit fully intact was indeed a miracle. Even the unpleasantness I remembered in perfect detail. What power, I thought, there is in the helmet of salvation spoken about in the letter to the Ephesians (Ephesians 6: 17) to ward off evil spirits seeking to run amok in a Christian's life. "Lord," I thought, "to as many as believe You do indeed give Your power to be victorious. You who search the heart know what is in the mind of the spirit. How true!!"

In spite of this tremendous preservation of mind by the Lord Himself, both Tina and I were aware how deeply entrenched the schizophrenia had been. It was becoming increasingly apparent to us the return to normal full freedom and wholeness of life was going to be a continuing process.

Tina had far more insight and revelation about the process than I had. She still observed that there was mental, emotional and spiritual ground yet to be recovered in my life, which she was expecting, but didn't envisage the fight to be so long. Though I was showing continuing signs of God's delivering and healing power in numerous ways, she expected me to move ahead at a faster pace.

She was encouraged, however, in observing my ability to relax more and find an ease in performing jobs. To both start and finish tasks immediately was a great contrast to past performances, which contained no perseverance or flexibility. This aspect of progress gave her hope when at other times she and others still observed some of the traits present before deliverance.

The demonic forces had built themselves so deeply into my thought patterns and behaviour that it was going to need my continual cooperation with the Holy Spirit to break the entrenchment for good.

To those helping schizophrenics back into normal living, the emphasis on the difficult job ahead is only too well known. Ida Mae Hammond says in her book *Pigs in the Parlour* that the schizophrenia deliverance is the deepest, most involved and most determined deliverance that she and her husband have encountered. It requires, they say, continuing cooperation with the Holy Spirit after deliverance and healing have taken place so that real wholeness in one's life may be established and enjoyed.

Ida Mae Hammond also says that it is hard work for the schizophrenic pressing through to full freedom. "I greatly admire schizophrenics who fight through to victory. I admire these victories above all other deliverances," she says.

These observations greatly encouraged me to continue seeking full restoration, and I wrote: "To be healed of a <u>physical disease</u> or condition means that you are restored to good and former physical health. To be healed of <u>schizophrenia</u> manifests firstly in the enjoyment of mental freedom once lost but now restored, and in the ability to function normally in everyday life hitherto acknowledged as a major impossibility."

Before being set free, I understood absolutely nothing about my illness of schizophrenia. I now had more insight into what is a very baffling problem to mental health professionals, for whom the cause and cure has remained shrouded in uncertainty. My priority had been in opposing its presence in my life and overcoming it through prayer. It became important to begin understanding the complexity of the illness in order to knock out the schizophrenic patterns completely, thereby making room for my true personality to come forth and replace it.

A revelation was given by the Lord to Ida Mae Hammond at a time she and her husband were helping a Christian woman earnestly desiring deliverance. God said to her: " 'Schizophrenia is a disturbance, distortion or disintegration of the development of the personality.' He instructed me to put my hands together, palms facing and with fingers laced together tightly. He said this represented what the schizophrenic nature was like. Each hand represented one of the dual personalities within the schizophrenic, neither of which was the real self. They were tightly interlocked. The Lord said: 'Your hands represent the nest of demon spirits that make up schizophrenia. I want you to know that it is demonic. It is a nest of demon spirits, and they came into this person's life when she was very, very young. I will show you how it operates'."

I saw only too plainly that the core of the schizophrenic was rejection and rebellion with the control demon called schizophrenia (or double-mindedness) which invites other demons in, in order to cause the distortion of the personality. When I read that it commonly begins in childhood or infancy and sometimes while the child is yet in his mother's womb, my mind flashed back to the knowledge that my mother wanted me to be a girl. I could accept that if the schizophrenia nature is in the mother then the illness could be demonically inherited as the demons pick out one or more of her children to feed down through. The rejection within herself creates problems in her relationships with the child who is exposed to rejection by the mother's instability.

I began comparing my healing and deliverance with that of the Gadarene paranoid demoniac recorded in Mark 5. He was a different type from the hebephrenic variety I was classed as. The third type is known as catatonic. I wondered if, where it is recorded that after Jesus had healed him and he was found "sitting there, dressed and in his right mind", it meant that the demoniac had not to go through any further process of restoration. How long had he had it? Was he a young man? Did Jesus complete deliverance, healing and restoration all in one go?

Tina and I talked this over time and time again. She came up with this explanation:

"I believe that when Jesus was on earth He healed all that were oppressed and every manner of sickness, as the Bible records. Because He was God in human form there was no restriction in any way to the operation of His power and authority. He himself indeed said: 'all power in heaven and earth is given to Me.' I believe that the Gadarene demoniac was delivered, healed and restored in one completed work all taking place at once."

She stated this knowing and believing at the same time that God had done a mighty, genuine work in deliverance and healing in my life — though the process of getting back into normalcy of living and wholeness for me would still be a continuing process.

Throughout the first seven months of my new freedom, I continued enjoying what was a new life. I recorded the following on New Year's Day, 1991:

"I am amazed how my suppressed emotions have been released since May Day. The best way to sum it up is to say: 'The Lord has done and is continuing to do a new thing.' I can now say that the same discipline which had been such a struggle to maintain before being set free, is now being maintained with a rest reigning in my heart. The only point I am having to watch at the moment, and in the future, is the need to address tiredness and fatigue which have always been a real enemy."

Observing my progress, Tina was now beginning to take seriously my proposal of marriage. Our relationship had always been subject to the will of God and I had made it clear to her that "I only wanted her if God brought her." She had always prayed about whether it was right to go ahead and get engaged in much the same way that my first wife Pam had done. How privileged I was that she too was seeking God for His answer.

She received guidance in prayer and was satisfied that it was right to proceed. While shopping in the town centre of Chesterfield for the engagement ring, we heard a local band playing "Amazing Grace". My mind flashed back to the time we included the hymn in our family contribution at a service at Zion Church in 1980. On hearing the words of the last verse, "When we've been there, ten thousand years, bright shining as the sun, we've no less days to sing God's praise than when we first began," I thought: "Lord, Pam has been with You almost ten years now. And she has no less days to spend with You than the day she passed into Your presence."

I also recalled her parting words on the last night before she died: "Jim, you should remarry for your sake and for the sake of the children." Here I was choosing an engagement ring for my second wife, whom I knew she would greatly approve of. One of the delights I am looking forward to on getting to heaven is to link up these two wonderful women God brought into my life. They both loved and cared for me and together helped me defeat the devil and all his fury and madness. It will be a glorious reunion in the presence of Jesus.

Having been set free I was now able to cooperate more with the Holy Spirit. The balanced truth of the word of God in demolishing satanic lies and footholds in my thought patterns became very

powerful. I readily agreed with Tina that I would benefit greatly from ministry and help from a professional Christian counsellor. We contacted Colin Nowell of Wholeness in Christ, who had left the Methodist ministry in order to have more time to minister to broken and shattered lives.

Colin first came to our house with a dear friend, David Bailey, the Baptist minister in Chesterfield, who was also involved in healing and deliverance. It proved such a profitable time that I knew it was right to continue seeing Colin at his home in Ecclesall, Sheffield. The ministry was carried out with the utmost consideration of being under the control of the Holy Spirit.

I was first asked how long a time I could cope with, as it was Colin's experience that people coming to him with schizophrenia could often only manage short spells of counselling and prayer. I agreed to a two or three hour session each time as my stickability since being set free had improved. I wanted to advance the good work God had begun.

The session with Colin moved my progress ahead quite significantly. I was pleased that contact with him came so close after being set free. Tina was more than delighted one day when she came along with me to the session to be introduced by Colin to a unique book, called *War on the Saints* by Jessie Penn Lewis with Evan Roberts, the Welsh revivalist. He advised us to obtain the full text unabridged edition, as the 'abridged' edition lost the content of the main thrust in eliminating important teaching regarding demonic influence on Christians. The editors of the first work based their decision to discontinue the original version "first and foremost" on their rejection that Christians could be demonised.

A copy of this work was soon in our hands and Tina began to devour its pages. She read how when believers receive the baptism in the Holy Spirit and the gifts of the Spirit they can sometimes enter into conflict with the powers of darkness and may discover the presence and activity of evil spirits already lurking in their lives. Such a discovery in unbelievers would be accepted, but it was "to the shock and even surprise for Christians to find it to be true."

When Jessie Penn-Lewis made this discovery, she was misunderstood and her teaching misinterpreted, hence the decision to "abridge" her work and so lose the main thrust of her book.

I was unable at first to see things contained in the work as clearly as Tina, but later agreed to the spiritual perception of Mrs Lewis' remarks considering how the baptism of the Holy Spirit in my life had disturbed an opposing presence.

Tina had in the early days of ministering to me given me spiritual indigestion when she introduced me to three volumes of *The Spiritual Man* by Watchman Nee, obtained during her days at Birmingham Bible Institute. She had tried, albeit in vain, to enlighten me with certain truths about the body, soul and spirit realm. Then, they were too deep for me to grasp. Certain truths were repeated in the books by both authors, though the treatment by each had its own particular slant.

Our engagement took place in May 1991, with the proposed wedding day being fixed for 19th October. Tina's father, Maurice, had only one reservation about our going ahead and that centred around my being able to keep up with Tina. But he had faith to see in future days that "God, who had begun a good work in healing, would attend to any deficiency", as he himself later witnessed.

In addition to wedding plans needing attention, there was the involvement with my brothers in caring for our mother. She was showing signs of not being able to look after herself in her new small flat. Her condition now warranted going into an old people's home, something she had asked us "not to do to her." An attractive proposition came along, however, to have a trial stay of six weeks in a newly-opened residential home located mid-way between myself and my brothers. She felt at home soon after being admitted and decided to stay.

In previous months, I had cut myself free from an ungodly soul tie of domination and control which my mother had over me. I continued visiting her, but there was not the same preoccupation with the need to be always making visits, which often left me emotionally sapped. Because she was not a "free" person I longed to lead her to a life-changing encounter with Christ, though she seemed unable to grasp my explanations of the love of God. There were times when I thought I was getting through. I prayed for her to see her need to receive Christ, but there was a life-long rejection and a root of bitterness which needed dealing with.

It was hard to minister adequately enough to show how her life had been blighted because of what had happened in childhood. Greater insight into all this was to dawn on me later on when she became senile and was unable to receive explanations.

Throughout her life, Mum had never broken free of the rejection which dogged her. Her desire for me to be a girl manifested itself later during a conversation with Tina, when in her deep confusion she said: "I'm having a baby girl."

Tina, always one to live in reality, faced her with things as they really were: "No, Mum Stacey, you're not! You have had three sons and the last one was James and I married him."

As though brought to her senses with a jolt, my mother then said: "Ah, yes."

It was a great relief, with a wedding ahead of us, to know that Mum was being cared for so we could apply ourselves to the seemingly gigantic task of planning all the arrangements with freedom.

I stirred at 5.45 a.m. on our memorable day, 19th October 1991, and had a leisurely start to what was going to be a great time of rejoicing. Many of the 175 guests attending the service at the Lye and Stambermill parish church, near Stourbridge, West Midlands, had been instrumental in praying me through, along with some of the 100 extra friends joining the evening reception. God's favour rested on the weather, as the sun shone throughout, making it an ideal occasion — though the days either side were weatherwise as different again.

When Tina arrived with her father to stand alongside me at the front of the church, she looked stunning. Whether the pale oyster dress with pearl buttons down the front was exactly the same version that I saw in a flash in the vision way back in 1988 raises an interesting question, but at least in appearance there was a resemblance. I continually thank God for the vision, without which I would not have pursued Tina and refused her decision to finish. Though not ready for marriage at the time it was given, I just knew God was planning something.

As I told Tina in a 15-verse birthday morning love-song that year:

"God saw me trying to secure
What I could not then discern
Midst mental blues and inward pain
I needed love again.

"I thought I'd never love again
And feel my heart-strings beat
The way they've done since I met you —
It's been God's special treat."

Tina and I on our Wedding Day, 1991

I could have used the first verse on our wedding-day, for I had so much gratitude in my heart:

> "I can't express on this special day
> My deep love for precious you.
> If my heart could be unlocked
> Its store would surprise you."

My deep joy was to see my children, my own mother, and my dear mother-in-law, Mum Horton, rejoicing in our happiness.

Having my own personal friends present who had known me during difficult periods of my life in and out of mental hospitals added to the joy. My former pastor, Rev Ernest Anderson, supported Rev David Woodhouse, the Vicar. David set the scene at the outset for a time of celebration and thanksgiving in the presence of God.

Tina's stepmother, Esther, caused a laugh as we boarded the wedding car. Having been alerted by Tina that the loops on the front of the dress were a little insecure, she drew near to the window and allayed any concern, saying:

"I've got me needle!"

Later Tina went into the ladies' room with her to have the loops attended to. Esther was a first-class seamstress, having made three of the four bridesmaids' dresses in deep pink oyster.

A barn dance brought the proceedings to a joyous climax. We finished up with "They shall go out with joy and be led forth with peace, and the mountains and the hills shall break forth before them."

It was a perfect end to a perfect day, and we all knew the Master of Ceremonies who had made our marriage possible!

11

Tina finds it hard to cope

We arrived back from honeymoon to start our married life in Chesterfield in the well-built, semi-detached Victorian home where I had lived since 1972. The fact that my illness had prevented me from keeping on top of many household jobs was something that soon became apparent to Tina now she had returned as the lady of the house. But the immediate crisis it caused was something I wish I could have avoided for her sake.

Neither of us felt completely fresh after our two weeks in Malta, nor were we equipped with a preparedness to launch into the thrill of what newly-marrieds are bursting to accomplish. Tina had more desire than I had in wanting to sort things out, but I lacked motivation because of tiredness.

She was used to rising to any occasion; however, discouragement soon set in when she saw I was unable to stand with her in applying myself to certain projects. Work commitment in Sheffield took almost all my strength, so that I had little left on reaching home to fire up any enthusiasm to start again. Little did I realise what was going on in Tina's mind and heart in those early days of marriage.

While going about the house, she found endless clutter of paperwork, magazines, sermon notes, and Mars bar wrappers intended for an offer never sent. In all this she saw "the schizophrenic mind" and the symptoms of a hoarding behavioural pattern.

She told me later: "I knew that if I had to wait to sit down with you and go through the enormous amount that I found in the cellar,

bedroom, wardrobe and cubbyhole, it would have taken endless time and you would have delayed the whole procedure. So while you were at work I sorted through everything and made several visits to the refuse tip with countless black bags. I kept the important personal things, such as Philip's birth certificate, but the majority had to go, as I would never have been able to cope otherwise."

The accumulation of all this backlog was only part of my problem. There were also the numerous, obvious irritations that showed the house had lacked DIY attention in the realm of basic improvements.

Take the front door, for example. Each time there was a caller, it was necessary to roll back the carpet over the uneven floor to open it the space of about eighteen inches. If you managed this without the heavy curtain behind the door crashing down on you, as the rail only rested on a large nail, then you were fortunate. The quick way out, of course, was to shout to callers to open the gate and go to the back door.

Another irritation was the need to use large paper clips on two of the four green patterned curtains stretching across the large bay window area. During courting days, this much-needed ingenuity to make sure the curtains closed properly was hilariously funny, but now the routine proved only to be frustrating.

I had done my best over the years to complete major projects. New attractive mahogany windows and secondary glazing in the lounge and front bedroom were a distinct feature, but there were a thousand and one items of evidence clear to the eye of neglect on my part — all because of my inability to get jobs done.

I was unaware that a bit of carpet in the bedroom fitted on the area bordering the main carpet smelt musty and needed removing, if only to give Tina the opportunity of sleeping better and so avoid her sneezing attacks.

When Tina failed to see the evidence she wanted of my having returned to normal life sooner than I did, it caused her frustration. I had been delivered and healed without doubt, but where was the much-needed evidence to show the mighty work God had really done?

We both realised that my healing was going to be progressive, with restoration coming gradually as my mind received strength. I

thought that in the same way a body takes time to recover after major surgery, so my mind, which had suffered prolonged intensive onslaught for 26 years, needed time to be fully restored. The healing started on May Day would need to continue and my personal freedom become more enlarged.

I was again cast on God for the wisdom of His grace at each and every turn. The wonder began to dawn on me that over my long illness I had been able to keep a job down, whereas a large majority of schizophrenics are unable to stir themselves to work, let alone remain constantly employed. I had done that for long years, even with the additional trauma of the major crisis of Pam's illness and losing her. The responsibilities, too, involved in bringing up my children afterwards, were carried out all without a major long recuperation.

A close friend told me: "I don't know how you have done it, Jim. If I were to lose my wife, that in itself would shatter me, but you lost yours and still had this horrendous illness to contend with. It must have been the Lord who has brought you through."

The crunch time for Tina arrived in the February just four months after our marriage. On a bitingly cold day, she had been without warmth in the house all day because of a problem with the central heating system. Arriving home, I found her crying, and felt concerned:

"I've had enough," she said. "I'm going home to Dad. I can't stand this any longer."

I replied: "OK, I'll come with you."

I comforted and consoled her for a long time and, as usual when anything used to go wrong or a difference occurred, we prayed together and gave the whole matter to the Lord. A crisis was averted that evening.

My main problem was still in the area of passivity. Tina was fully expecting further advance in the mental, emotional and spiritual areas, but she didn't envisage the fight to be so long and arduous. I failed to grasp at times the amount of passivity that still needed breaking in my life; how deeply the demonic forces had built themselves into my personality, creating a passivity which the power of faith and prayer continually needed to smash.

I was often agitated, causing Tina concern on numerous occasions. She began keeping a diary of everything going on that was a problem area. It helped in her prayer times for me to focus on needs urgently requiring to be dealt with.

The first entry on May 19th records:

"James and I went for a walk around the dam. Also had a good talk. I explained the teaching again in 'Pigs in the Parlour' and that he would have to respond to challenge when he was oppressed. He agreed. He seemed very released and happy. On coming home I made us a drink, did his sandwiches, then went upstairs at 9.45 p.m. I read a portion out loud but James was very sleepy by then.

"I had my side light on and wanted to read but James became very agitated. He fell asleep and at 10.15 p.m. the phone went and woke him up. He became restless and agitated, so I went into another bed at 10.50 p.m. to read and came back later when I felt sleepy. It looks as though James can't even stand a side light on. What do I do? Gone are the days of reading in bed!"

May 20th:

"Got up late. I always feel tired when James is agitated — it seems to affect me. Had a good time of prayer. The Lord seemed to be telling me to resist satan. The more we resist and stand firm the stronger we'll become. Galatians 5: 1 'It is for freedom that Christ has set us free. Stand firm, then, and do not let yourselves be burdened again by a yoke of slavery.' The more one has been in bondage the more one has to stand firm against the enemy as he seeks again and again to oppress us. He will tire after a while."

The entry a few days later drew attention to my waking habits. Tina observed that on a Sunday morning I was up at 4.30.

"He felt he had to get out. Sometimes, I feel he's being pushed by a restless spirit, and it certainly has an effect on me!! We must keep praying about this sleep pattern. Joan (Clark) phoned Sunday evening — just like a breath of fresh air. We

chatted half an hour. We must get together the end of June for a few days of prayer."

By this time, Tina was beginning to make a difference in the house. She had already decorated the living-room with attractive wallpaper and had put up made-to-measure curtains. Maurice and Esther could see she was making a pleasant impact. Her diary continues:

"After waving them off, James went upstairs to the bathroom to get ready for the praise and prayer meeting at church, but came down feeling very tired and slightly agitated. He lay on the floor in the living room and I suggested that if he was so tired perhaps he should rest. After that we had our reading and prayer time. I felt led to pray and wait on the Lord. The only thing I felt strongly coming from the Lord was to ask James: 'Did your mother have difficulty in sleeping?'

"He said she had great difficulty sleeping all her life. This is also another strong bondage coming down the family line. We prayed against spirits of insomnia, nervousness. His knee seemed better afterwards with less restriction. He slept better, but was up at 5 a.m."

The continuing reliance on close friends who were willing to pray was a great support to Tina, such as the break spent with Joan and Robin Clark at Clitheroe. The diary entry records:

"We realised James showed signs in his behaviour of the following:
1. ritualism — getting up and going to bed at certain times, washing of hair daily;
2. doctrinal obsession — revival, getting into a ministry and prayer
3. mysticism — seeing everything in spiritual terms, and a lack of interest in the natural. I felt, because of this emphasis on the spiritual without an outlet of the natural, he therefore becomes tired and lethargic. Has this spirit brought in spirits of insomnia, and lethargy, fatigue?

4. fear — sometimes fearful in certain situations.
5. victim — spirit of victim. We all felt a unity in feeling the above were James. The Lord gave me Ephesians 1 verses 17,18 to pray for James for ... 'a spirit of wisdom and revelation'. We prayed for him to recognise his need."

On her return, I asked Tina how she had been led to pray with Joan and Robin. My favourable, grateful response caused her to write in her diary: "He accepted what we felt the Lord had shown us. Miracle!!"

There were times when I thought Tina had not always discerned correctly in her assessment of me. Throughout our relationship, I had wanted her to keep on challenging me about everything she thought was not right. Since being freed I tended at times to think I had received all I needed to know about myself, perhaps denying at times that I was still on the road to wholeness.

Sometimes when she observed me a "little sleepy" in a meeting, I would make the excuse that "anyone who gets up as early as I do will certainly feel sleepy". On one occasion she pointed it out at a day conference at St. Thomas' and I was perhaps less than kind in saying that I thought she "had a spirit of criticism." I was sad to read later in her diary:

"I was upset and felt he didn't understand at all. He got out of bed to sleep on the floor but I just sobbed quietly. I felt tired and up against a lot of deceit. Eventually he came to bed."

These little disagreements really tired Tina out. She was still suffering from irritable bowel syndrome for which the doctor had prescribed Regulan. It seemed that her tiredness always increased when I refused her challenges and insisted on my line of argument. She called round to see some Pentecostal friends, Tom and Cath Steer, near our home and was encouraged to "slow down" and enjoy our new life.

Tina's ability to keep helping me stemmed from her periodic times of prayer and waiting on God. An entry on July 7th gives a

little insight:

> "Time of prayer; tried to analyse the relationship between waiting on God for revelation and intercessory prayer. Worship, Thanksgiving, Listening (hearing God's voice) and Intercession are so important — the first three fire faith into the heart for the fourth."

We had decided a long time earlier that in time Tina would look for a job as a practice nurse at a local doctor's surgery. After a successful interview, however, she felt quite depressed about having to go back to work, since she was rather overwhelmed at the prospect of taking responsibility and doing further courses again. But she only spent a short time in that job.

During a holiday in Eastbourne in mid-July 1992 shared with Maurice and Esther, I felt inspired to start writing about my healing and deliverance. Having worked as a journalist I knew what made a good story. My testimony had not only one single human interest attraction, but three.

Firstly, the romantic aspect — joining a dating agency, and marrying the woman who brought me through my illness — had sufficient appeal in itself. Secondly, an up-to-date account of deliverance from schizophrenia at a time in our modern culture when the illness is such an area of concern. Thirdly, God providing the answer to some in the Church who say that Christians cannot be demonised. I knew the story was dynamite. I longed to get it out — but it was going to have to keep for a few years to be able to write the sequel about my full return to wholeness, and detailing the steps along the way in order that others may be helped.

As days progressed, my inability to rest properly and have refreshing sleep was a mystifying problem to Tina. She recorded in her diary the numerous times when I told her I had not slept properly:

"If he gets slightly overtired and goes to bed after 10 p.m, (even half an hour later) he seems unable to sleep and becomes very restless. Most people sleep quicker and deeper if they are tired unless they are exhausted following a very tiring and unusual regime."

Coupled with this tiredness was the desire to have time on my own. Often when in company, I would not want to stop and chat with people, say after a church service. Tina noted: "I wonder if this is the rejection side of his personality emerging? I don't know, but when he's like this, I feel oppressed."

Further progress in moving forward in being able to discern my condition was made during the visit of Tina's "auntie", Elsie Circuit, from Higher Blackley in Manchester. Elsie, a retired spinster, had been wonderfully converted through the help given by Tina's mother during the time of her father's ministry in the city. A friendship had developed over the years, and since she lacked the opportunity to have a holiday, Tina fetched her by car to Chesterfield.

She was particularly gifted in DIY through having to run her own home. Keen to see improvements move ahead in the house, she helped Tina paint the skirting board on the landing and staircase in preparation for the carpet being laid. With all three of us working together, we took the heavy front door off its hinges and shaved inches off the bottom so that it could ride over the carpet.

Although there were definite breakthroughs in my life, as Tina's diary shows, she was still looking for a swifter return to normalcy. The way to restoration was not going to be achieved quickly but would be a long sequence of gradual improvements, as thought patterns fashioned in my mind by the demons left me for good.

The onslaught of the religious spirit had left an embroiled imprint in my mind. I had always wanted to be in full-time Christian work, an ideal I still cherished after our wedding. At work there had been numerous men taking early voluntary retirement in recent months, and I was considering joining the leavers since I was turned

50. On the first Sunday in September, 1992, I told Tina I was not going to church because I wanted to pray about my employment.

Observing my withdrawn face, she replied: "If the Lord had wanted you to do that He would have given you warning, allowing you to plan a special time of prayer beforehand."

Noting the incident in her diary, she recorded: "I had quite a spiritual battle. He agreed to come to church and in fact was blessed through the service."

Her entry continued:

"When he returned home, he said he had been glad he didn't 'go inward' or something like that. James was quite irritated at little things as I was getting the dinner ready. I realised that this was not him. We had visited his mother in the nursing home the previous day, and nearly every time he visits her there is a reaction afterwards. James apologised for his awkward irritability and after lunch he helped me wash up. I then encouraged him to go to bed and sleep. I then started writing my diary and realised I must get down to prayer for James. Have the soul ties between him and his mother really been broken?

"At 4.45 p.m., James was still in bed, and I discerned that this was definitely not a normal tiredness. Another bout of abnormal behaviour was to follow after he came downstairs and found me in the living room praying. This made him irritated. I heard him speaking in the front room and presumed he was on the telephone to someone. I carried on praying in tongues and realised I was up against something. This went on for half-an-hour or so. Most of my time was spent in worship and claiming the power of the blood of Jesus.

"James eventually came back into the room to join me, this time he was in a receptive mood and began to worship with me. However, as I continued praying in tongues I felt God say that James' family spirits were still in operation. The main demonic

force has been cut off from the roots but still there are others hanging on. James then began to assert his will and as soon as he did that, he realised he was still suffering 'domination' from his mother. We prayed against domination, rebellion, witchcraft, rejection and irritability."

Tina then anointed me with oil and prayed, and we felt the oppression gradually leave. I realised there had been something operating in me when I had felt resentment welling up during the prayer time.

I agreed with Tina that there had been cynicism too. After prayer we went to church. She concluded this entry in her diary with an assessment that I was still being *oppressed*, though not *possessed* by certain spirits:

" ... when these ... rear their heads they have to be challenged. The difficulty is that he is blinded to the fact and often unable to discern when he is oppressed. I must keep coming, praying etc., until the hold of these spirits completely leaves him. What does the Lord want me to do on a regular level to achieve that end? Fast and pray once a week?"

Looking through Tina's diary years later, I was full of admiration for the way she kept on with the commitment to help me become completely free.

"I'm so glad I kept that record of how difficult it was even after deliverance and healing," she told me.

At the heart of everything was her faith to believe that the power of Jesus Christ would fully restore me, a belief that I shared. It was a long road, but we were getting there!

Esther and Maurice with Tina and myself.

12

Passivity begins to lose its hold

Life continued at a busy pace, with numerous commitments and changes, which meant that the focus on moving towards full restoration had to be sought amidst the routine of normal everyday activities. We also needed continuing adjustment to married life. Tina needed time to settle down and make new friendships at St. Thomas' parish church opposite our home. I was grateful that in the months preceding April, 1993, my administration job in Datapost at Royal Mail was coming to an end, giving times free of pressure during the winding-down period.

A fresh challenge awaited me in a new job working in the Investigation Branch. It came during staff change in the business when my new boss moved from West Yorkshire. We began as a completely new team with me offering support in areas addressing internal fraud among postmen. The work demanded a new commitment in relations and performance, which I was determined to succeed in.

Our office backed onto the main road above the sorting office near Fitzalan Square in Sheffield and provided ample room, a feature which was most pleasing. We had the run of the place to ourselves, apart from a small room where a colleague from the Post Office Investigation Department sat. In a short time, we moved into an adjoining room almost twice as big and revelled in even more spaciousness.

In June, I had a major breakthrough while out enjoying a picnic in the Derbyshire countryside with Tina on realising the important need of spiritual alertness in order to remain free. After stopping the

car to have lunch, a deep, abnormal tiredness settled over me. I discerned it was an evil presence oppressing me and resembled more of a slumbering condition inducing passivity and lethargy which sought to totally inactivate me.

After finishing our picnic, I sensed a heaviness over and around my eyes and was unable to enjoy the brilliant sunshine. I told Tina of my need to pray. She joined me in commanding the heaviness to leave in Jesus' name. Within minutes, I became free of the oppressive state.

This same problem had also occurred the previous Sunday in the same location but to a lesser extent. Chesterfield is well known for occult influence and there may have been an influence in the area where we were visiting. Nevertheless, I realised the need for spiritual alertness and wrote down three important principles:

a.   the necessity of having a living, conscious faith
b.   the continual need of remaining alert through
     jealously guarding my spirit (remember the benefits of
     keeping the law of faith)
c.   the need to guard against those things that sap spiritual
     power and cause me to go "flat" inside.

I noted there was a link in some way between the condition here detailed and the uneasy fear I showed in relation to wanting to go to bed early in order to secure adequate sleep. Before deliverance and healing, the fight towards freedom proved long and intense. I had to drive my will inside the schizophrenia prison to get up to pray in order to be spiritually prepared for the day and keep up the warfare being waged.

The whole incident inspired the thought that I needed further counselling and prayer concentration to hit the inner core of my mind. Only then would there be complete restoration to wholeness and soundness. In other words, more power was needed to break the passivity and the patterns still formed in my mind left by the now exorcised spirits.

I wrote the whole incident down, showed Tina the details and she commented:

"My, your perception of yourself has grown. You wouldn't

have been able to see that a year ago."

Being able to see myself more clearly was attributable to nothing less than another breakthrough in prayer. In recent months Tina had prayed for God to give me more revelation about myself.

Her diary made the comment way back in September:

"He is seeing himself more clearly but still not able to see himself as others do. This inertia/passivity seems to sap a lot of his energy. I know that the withdrawn side will still keep reasserting itself. How is this stronghold going to be completely cut? We've not prayed against withdrawal, unreality, fantasy, escape, sleepiness, passivity."

Another wonderful answer to prayer along the way! I began to observe other advances in gaining natural strength and relaxation. I was now sleeping a lot better, even sometimes dropping off during the journey to work and waking up when the bus pulled up with a jolt at the Sheffield terminus. Considering the backlog of years when I never used to secure adequate rest and relaxation, I was grateful for every improvement in sleep and rest. My body needed exercise, since I had not taken part in sports or regular walks for so long.

Completing several widths at the swimming baths really loosened up my frame, with the added joy of beating Tina in racing across.

I was by no means free of tiredness, however. Having to be out of the house at 7 a.m. for work meant rising at 5.30 or 5.45 in order to meet God in prayer. I arrived back home at 17.30, which meant a full day five days a week. A weakness I had was that if tired, I saw the need to be quiet and avoid noise of any sort. Tina, who had needed to adjust to noisy music through the night in the heart of Bombay in her missionary days, used to suggest that whatever the noise I should be able to handle it. But my inability to do so revealed that I couldn't switch off in a given situation.

In the summer of 1993, Tina became quite down and tired. She had various blood tests and her doctor thought she was depressed due to the menopause. He proved right in part, but she had severe pains in her arms radiating down to her hands. Many a time during the

111

night the cramps were unbearable. Then she saw that her elbows were beginning to swell.

Tina's problem with her joints dates back to the time when she was four years old and fell from a first floor window at her grandparents' home near Morecambe, landing on her knees on a concrete yard. The impact then caused her to fall forward, hitting her head on the concrete, resulting in a large egg-shaped lump on her forehead.

She speaks of being miraculously preserved, for in the seconds as she was falling from the window, she noticed a split-second white flash. She believed it to be an angel who had intervened at the point of falling. The local doctor, on being phoned to come to the house, was unwilling at first because only recently he had attended a young girl in a nearby street who had fallen to her death in just the same way.

As for myself, I still kept seeing the need for further counselling and ministry, and arranged another session with Colin Nowells, supported by Tina in November 1993. Little did I realise beforehand, the magnitude of another advance soon to be made in the area concerning my mother's desire of wanting me to be a girl.

Colin discerned that I had not wanted to be born and had turned my back on life while in the womb. During a time of waiting before God, I confessed that I had "not wanted to come out into the world and be born."

Colin believed that I had also said: "I'm not going to be born".

I confessed this as sin, was anointed with oil and prayed "to be born and choose life."

Following the above ministry, I seemed to have a new lease of life until it was agreed to pray into the next agenda with Colin in the area of tiredness and lethargy. Tina wondered if the problem was linked to family spirits of passivity. She recorded:

"They are evident in the family and particularly in James. James may have received passivity in the womb, but he also prayed for six months with an empty mind when he was specifically seeking guidance for future ministry.

"Is this tiredness due to the passivity in action? He always makes excuses for the tiredness e.g. by saying: 'Anyone doing what I'm doing would be tired, and would naturally get tired

more easily. It's only natural to be tired like this. I'm not getting any younger' etc."

While it was perfectly clear to Tina and Colin that some time would be needed for the passivity to be dealt with through asserting my will, it was not obvious to me because I couldn't see myself as clearly as they could. I really needed to take stock of what Tina was always pointing out to me about Normalcy Recognised, a section dealt with clearly by Chinese author, Watchman Nee, in his book *The Spiritual Man*. I may have read the following but it had not gripped me. It makes vital reading for anyone seeking to help a schizophrenic and knowing what is involved.

In Volume 3, he writes:

"If one has plunged into all sorts of vexations due to passivity or believing the lies of the evil spirits, he urgently needs to determine what is normal for him. Except for the unrenewed mind, both passivity and assent to lies furnish such footholds to evil spirits that the Christian's mental state will deteriorate steadily in every direction.

"His powers of recall, of physical endurance, and so forth will all continually fail. If he realises his danger he ought to rise up and seek liberation. But what should be regarded as liberation? It is this ... he needs to be restored to his original state. It's essential for anyone who seeks restoration to determine what his original state was. Each person has his normal condition, the state he had before his illness. He must be made aware of his normal state. He should therefore ask himself these questions:

1. What was my former condition?
2. How far am I today from it?
3. How can I be restored to it?

"Your former state is your normal state. The condition from which you fell is your measuring rod should you be ignorant of what is normal for you — you need to ask:

1. Was my mind born so confused or was there a time

when I was not confused?

2.   Was I always so sleepless or did I once sleep well?

3.   Did I always have so many pictures passing before my eyes like movies on a screen or were there some clear moments?

4.   Have I always been weak or was there a time when I was stronger?

5.   Is it true I never could control myself or could I once manage myself much better?

"By answering these questions the person ought to be able to perceive whether he lacks his normal state, is under attack, has grown passive.   To define what his original condition was a person must acknowledge and believe initially that HE DOES have a normal state."

The ministry with Colin became difficult for me during the times I was restless and uneasy.   Tina felt a hardness of evil spirit activity in the session, but prayer was offered into passivity of family line spirits.

As the subject of "Normalcy Recognised" was being discussed, Colin discerned that I was not accepting it.   Some old thought patterns came out in conversation.   Tina recorded in her diary:

"We came away feeling tired (at least I did).   I was tempted to give up and begin to think about living my own life because of James's tremendous pull on me.   He's very draining when the opposition (in spirit) rises up and his mind on some levels is very deceived.   It was obvious Colin discerned that.   Now the Lord reminded me of Psalm 71 verse 14: 'But as for me, I shall always have hope.   I will praise you more and more'. "

As the months went by, I knew my inner life was getting stronger.   I wanted to succeed in relationships with colleagues in the Investigation Branch and provide them with every support in carrying out the difficult task of detecting fraud.   There was always plenty of work in the "melting pot" with ongoing suspects being watched; but everything was eclipsed when in the autumn of 1993, Sheffield encountered the first murder of a postman in the 350 years'

history of the Post Office.

A long-serving postman driver had been run over and killed as he tried to prevent his van being stolen while clearing a pillar box. The descent of police into our office and the length and extent of the enquiry for many months exacted a commitment in support work. During a house-to-house search in the south of Sheffield, police discovered a large amount of mail in a garage which a former postman had not wanted to deliver and hidden away. Every item of mail had to be recorded in this "side issue", as well as helping out with the major enquiry.

Tina and I were maintaining an interest in healing and deliverance, though I needed to have a proper respect for the power of satan and demons. Although experiencing the effectiveness of the power of the blood of Jesus Christ in my life, I still had important lessons to learn.

Before getting involved in praying for deliverance for others, I must be living in the power of the Spirit and protected by Christ. Demons given legal rights do not leave people without being handled and addressed properly. Even God has to acknowledge the areas where demons have been given legal rights to be. So there was need for empowered living with Christ.

This insight came home with real force during a time of prayer for deliverance for Tina. She often complained of abdominal pain which I thought was associated with witchcraft in her family line from a previous generation. Without protecting myself adequately, and praying in the name of Jesus, I proceeded to take authority over the evil presence and immediately suffered a backlash. I was hit with such power in my head, falling backwards and hitting the floor with a bump. I gathered myself, got up and said to Tina: "I was not fully protected then. That's taught me a lesson."

I realised I didn't know everything about satan and his kingdom of darkness. I needed to see, as one author puts it, that "experience is needed to give life to the study but study is necessary to give sense and meaning to the experience."

An opportunity occurred in December 1993 of helping a friend from church who had suffered untold abuse from her parents involved in satanism. At first, I feared the commitment would be too much. It was, however, to prove an enriching experience and

115

privilege to minister the love of Jesus into her life without focusing on deliverance.

When Tina rang me at work to ask if I was in agreement that our friend and her fiancé stay in our home to give them a break, I said I needed more time to think about it. Tina was somewhat disappointed, to say the least, although I finally agreed to their coming.

Our friend had been found in a state of neglect in her flat one day by a neighbour who later fell in love with her. He helped her back to improved health and strength. Her background was one of being brought up in a satanic coven which had deeply entrenched spiritual, emotional and physical repercussions. As it is so needful to minister the love of Jesus to broken lives, we just made them feel at home.

Tina went to great pains to give them really good meals and express the love of Jesus in a relaxed setting. As our friend had been deprived of love in her family home, we sat with them to watch the video, "Anne of Avonlea."

She remarked to Tina: "So that's what family life is all about."

Tina's big heart went out in loving compassion, even to the point of dressing her up in her wedding gown in readiness for the proposed marriage they were planning.

The presence of cancer, however, prevented her reaching the wedding day. She was willing for God to heal her, but having suffered such immense trauma was now ready to go home to be with Jesus. Her life account told of horrific happenings which had left her so scarred, battered and bruised. We prayed a great deal for her, as did her friends at church. She finally went into a local hospice to spend her remaining days. We were glad, however, to have offered the love of Jesus at the close of her life.

The funeral was so unusually joyous. Pastor David Bailey, minister, told us that she had said "it was to be party and celebration because she was going home to be with Jesus." We were exhorted to rejoice for her, that having suffered so much, she had found her precious Saviour who had seen it right to take her home to be with Him. It was a most moving occasion, with tears filling many eyes.

13

Delivered to declare

During early 1994, I began to make major strides in picking up the broken pieces of my life. I thought it would be good to start telling my testimony of God's delivering and healing power, but was immediately aware of how many would view my story with scepticism. To speak about being healed of cancer or a visible illness would be more easily received than speaking about conquering a mental illness, particularly schizophrenia.

Any thought of moving ahead with that idea, however, had to be shelved when in the same week of making plans for Maurice's 80th birthday party his wife, Esther, died suddenly in hospital after suffering a massive heart attack. Tina and I were immediately thrown into offering our support with funeral arrangements and helping Maurice face the future without her.

We had disclosed to them the previous summer our intention of coming to live in Halesowen. Now it seemed that the choice was something we would have to make much sooner than anticipated. Maurice could have come to live with us in Chesterfield, but we knew that uprooting him at his time of life would present difficulties.

We soon made up our mind to put our house up for sale in the Spring and began seeking a house in Halesowen. First enquiries were on a property just four houses down on the opposite side of the road where Maurice lived. It was at first an attractive proposition. Later, when pressed to make a decision about buying, we had to forsake our interest because we ourselves needed a buyer.

Selling houses in Chesterfield was generally slow at that time. We decided to seek to buy the rented house from the Church of

117

England Pension Board where Maurice had lived since retiring. By the end of one whole year without there being a sale on our home, we were not only becoming a little discouraged, but very weary in keeping two homes going. Tina and I were separated very often.

Planning to live in Halesowen would entail a job transfer to Royal Mail, Birmingham. In the past, it was possible to get a transfer without any problem, but now the procedure meant that every vacancy had to be advertised, allowing open competition with others to win any job. I travelled down to Birmingham three times for interviews without success. I was fairly optimistic about getting a job in the Security Section, but failed.

There was a need to pass my driving test for the car in order to help Tina with the added responsibility of caring for Maurice. I had first begun taking lessons over six years earlier simply to impress her. Tina passed her test at the second attempt and was not expecting me to get through first time. But I surprised her.

On the day of the test, walking back to the Department of Transport waiting room, where she had just left to meet me, I shouted at a distance, with the "L" signs held high:

"I've made it!"

She replied: "That's wonderful! But I never expected it!"

Since Tina was now spending a good deal of time in Halesowen caring for her father, we decided that in order for her to keep up to date with practice nursing she would work three days a week at a surgery in Birmingham.

During the days apart, I began writing my testimony after arriving home from work. I came across the video testimony of Ian McCormack, a New Zealander, who had been miraculously saved after being bitten by a poisonous fish. I contacted the man who had produced the video and he was excited about doing my story.

In spite of mounting pressures of daily life, I knew the importance of continually turning to the Bible for inner strength. I could best pray and continue in prayer for a good length of time after first nourishing my spirit through meditating on the word of God. I would take great delight in seizing a fresh verse of Scripture, memorise it, and then use it for regular meditation. It enabled me to keep my mind from being overloaded and being bogged down.

We wanted some movement in the sale of our house and were

not relishing spending another winter under the same arrangement.

Tina said to me on the last day of April, 1995, as we returned home to Chesterfield from Halesowen: "I'm really getting emotionally tired with being in two places."

On arriving home, she never had a minute through catching up on chores; washing; cleaning; shopping and gardening. It was a routine carried out at both houses and was proving too much.

We were both getting very tired. Though I continued getting stronger, I realised that circumstances were causing increased pressure, and with the constant daily travelling to work during the week and going down to Halesowen at the weekend, tiredness seemed to be always increasing. Then we received the news that my brother Ian was suffering from incurable cancer. Through praying, we found inner strength to cope with this ourselves, as well as being able to minister to him, his wife and family.

We decided to have a real time of intercession asking God to bring along a buyer. Just after the first week in June, someone showed a marked interest in wanting to purchase our home. No doubt the new kitchen which my future son-in-law had installed and the improvements Tina had brought to the house were major factors in making the property attractive.

At last things moved ahead, and after securing the arrangement to buy the property in Halesowen, we moved out of Chatsworth Road on August 5th. It was a family affair with Tina's nephews arriving in the removal van, helping to load up and eventually travel down the well-worn route of the A38 to our new home.

I then had to begin travelling to work in Sheffield on a Monday morning from Birmingham, returning home on a Friday. I had a variety of places to stay overnight, including the YMCA, bed and breakfast accommodation and with my aged mother-in-law. The condition of my brother was progressively getting worse, and I was greatly burdened for him, feeling the need to visit him in the evenings after work. His eventual passing in September 1995 was both a great blow, and emotionally draining.

I now realised the need to pull out all the stops to secure a job in Birmingham by contacting the Personnel Manager, the Employee Support Manager and even asking the help of the Communication Workers' Union.

A rapid response came in a call from Personnel: "There's a job going in Birmingham Royal Mail in the Security Section. Can you get down there on Wednesday morning for an interview?"

As I was now residing in Halesowen, I was able to say: "It's no problem."

I was much happier about this second try for a job in the Security Section. It was in the Investigation branch and didn't concern working on the security of buildings and property like the previous vacancy. I was up early to ask God to help me with the interview, and the personal word of encouragement received in my Bible reading was:

"This day you will cross over this Jordan."

I had a good interview and was soon informed that I was preferred to others much younger than myself from the Birmingham office itself.

My days in Sheffield, where I had worked for nearly nine years, came to an end early December 1995, but not before I had put on a farewell buffet for my colleagues with whom I had enjoyed working. I was so pleased that my boss, with whom I had worked very well, wrote a good appraisal in my annual report. The work had certainly presented a challenge, but one I had only been able to fulfil because of increased mental strength.

So a new era started at Royal Mail, Birmingham, the largest sorting office in Europe, where because of its size I fully expected my workload and responsibility to increase. After first getting used to the new environment, I got the impression that my managers felt they could trust me to get on with the work. They were happy that I was there to give them my utmost cooperation. My healing was being tested in the pressure of a busy office throughout the day, and later in getting acclimatised to living in a new area.

I didn't think it was right to mention when first starting work in Birmingham anything about my healing. Imagine the effect of disclosing that the man they had recently welcomed into their ranks had been a schizophrenic for 26 years! When the pressure of work was really on at times, I felt satan taunt me that the news about the schizophrenia problem was getting out. But I kept completely silent about the illness that had dogged my life.

The amount of commitment in my first weeks in Birmingham

leading up to Christmas, which, of course, is the busiest time of the year in Royal Mail, was very heavy indeed.

I was so glad to reach the few days holiday to recover from a most exacting time. I was getting stronger, true, but in my heart hoped the kind of pressure experienced in my initial period was not going to be as heavy all the year through. Again, the power of prayer sustained me, kept me steady on course, and gradually rebuilt the areas of my life which needed to become even stronger.

The year 1996 was not many days old when another major pressure was to hit us. My elder brother, Keith, who had been suffering with a heavy cough prior to Christmas, was also diagnosed with cancer. Here was another test for my healing. I was in a sense "being pressed out of measure and pressed to all length". I knew the strength which comes through communion with Christ and was not going to allow this second, sudden family pressure to overcome me.

I readily made myself available to my brother and his family, and was on hand to offer support right up to the time of his death in May. These were indeed days of constant emotional strain which would have been hard to handle except for the fact that I was now more able to receive God's grace for strengthening.

To put it mildly, Tina and I were being stretched in a great many directions. We managed to get off on a prepared holiday to mid-Wales early May. We travelled to north Nottinghamshire to attend the funeral mid-week and then returned to the seaside resort to finish our break. The few days were needful in providing a measure of rest for us.

It was a great test, when visiting my mother in the nursing home, deciding it was best because of increasing senility not to tell her of my brother's passing. We had decided not to inform her about Ian's passing the previous September, as she would have been unable to bear it. But now to go and see her on the funeral day of my elder brother, Keith, without being able to mention his passing was something I found very difficult. Seeing my family with me that day, I think Mum sensed something just for a brief moment when she exclaimed, "Oh no!!", without adding more.

The emotional impact of losing two brothers within eight months completely drained me. I was cast again on God for strength. But another blow was to hit me within six weeks of the funeral when

121

my mother passed away.

Emptying her neat and attractive room where she had been so happy and well looked after for nearly six years was a most difficult assignment. It tested my healing again, but I knew that if life, with its trials and difficulties, had something more just around the corner to wear me down, I would fight through in faith.

Despite the succession of bereavements and an increasing workload at Royal Mail, I gradually began to regain my emotional and mental strength. The desire to share my testimony seemed important, though Tina suggested I wait a bit longer. I invited a couple of Christians to my home to interview me about my story, though on the day they arrived my careful preparation was put on one side and I just sat and told my details off the cuff. The video proved to be a blessing to several people, though in some areas it could have been better presented. But I was happy in telling what God had done for me. It strengthened me in declaring His faithfulness.

Not long afterwards, I felt the call of God return to preach. I had not delivered a sermon since the summer of 1987, but I knew it was right to follow the Holy Spirit's promptings. I saw my vicar, the Rev David Woodhouse, to say that I was not pushing myself in any way but was convinced of the guidance to start preaching again. David listened most attentively, and it was not long before I was appearing on the church rota.

It was most encouraging after finishing my first sermon, when having asked the congregation for a little indulgence until "I got the wheels oiled again," a friend said something to the effect: "Take my word for it, the wheels are well oiled already."

I soon became aware during the times of sermon preparation how different my preaching had become. For many years prior to healing, I had often depended on the sermons of others instead of being able, because of my mental problems, to preach something of my own. I now felt free to present my own material and could write it up on the cheap computer with an amazing freedom. How liberating it was to preach truths which the Holy Spirit had revealed to me. I no longer needed the sermons of Dr William Sangster of Westminster Central Hall, some of which I could preach verbatim from memory, or those I had written down in the chapel during my

time at Cliff College.

I was now free to preach the relevant freedom offered by Jesus which strengthened faith. I had a message to proclaim backed home by God's faithfulness and love which nobody could deny. I would often bring into my messages some personal illustration from my struggles, but was careful to point out that I was not always going to be using the time of ministry just to "peddle my own testimony." I was determined always to preach and offer Christ, and nothing thrilled me more than when at one service an 80-year-old friend in our church walked to the front to ask me to lead her to Christ. He was honouring His word, and that was a great encouragement.

During the autumn of 1996, Tina and I were approached to be the prayer co-ordinators at Christ Church the Lye and Stambermill, and agreed to serve. It was a demanding appointment, since we discerned that the area of Lye needed a spiritual breakthrough. The atmosphere inside our church itself had been affected over the years by freemasonry making it difficult to preach the word of God with liberty, and it was hard for people to come into real spiritual freedom. In hindsight, the appointment was too early for me in that it impeded at times the spiritual progress and pathway to wholeness I was seeking. We struggled for two years in the job before resigning, but felt that our contribution had made some impact.

The desire to release my story to the well-known Christian monthly magazine, *Renewal,* was backed up by a letter from my minister, David. I was aware how much the letter of support was needed, particularly when I was claiming a "self-certified" healing. David wrote saying that he had witnessed the increasing freedom in my life received through healing and deliverance.

He went on:

"James and Tina were members of Christ Church when I arrived in April 1991. I had the privilege of marrying them later in the year. Five years later he is beginning to take positions in the Church through House Group leadership with Tina, preaching on Sundays and from a deep commitment to prayer. James' story shows the powerfulness of a loving God who responds to our searching for a deep salvation. Not everyone may come by the same route into healing, but God is faithful to

us whatever the circumstances and the outcome. I commend his story as one example of the healing Jesus Christ offers to us today, bringing hope out of darkness."

The reply from Wallace Boulton, editor of *Renewal*, was that he thought the testimony more suitable for the sister publication, *Healing and Wholeness*. There was no response from this quarter, which brought a little disappointment. It did prepare me, however, for what I considered to be the standard reaction in some quarters of Christian publications towards mental healing. I was to have greater encouragement with a short article and photograph sent to the *New Life* newspaper, for which I used to write years before.

It was a great encouragement to receive the comments of two former Pentecostal pastors in Chesterfield who had known me during the times of real setback in my illness. George Parrott, now at Luton Pentecostal Church, wrote to say:

"It was good to hear from you, and thank you so much for your video of the wonderful healing that has taken place in your life. We give glory to God for His goodness, and have passed it on to others to see. As you say we were not into this kind of ministry some years back, but I, too, have seen new light from the Scriptures and through personal experience with Christians have, of course, altered my opinion."

Pastor Ernest Anderson, and his wife, Joan, who had supported me during my final spells in the psychiatric ward in Chesterfield, added their support:

"We welcomed the opportunity of seeing and hearing your witness of God's goodness. It was most heartening and we were delighted over what the Lord has done. To Him be all the glory! He is worthy of all the praise."

Through talking with a medical consultant who attended our church, I accepted his suggestion of obtaining some support for my healing from the psychiatric field. This caused me to make enquiries to locate the psychiatrist in Sheffield who had first dealt with me on

a regular footing when my illness first emerged in the mid-1960s.

Dr Neville Gittleson could scarcely remember me so far back meeting him at Mexborough Montagu Hospital and Sheffield Hospitals, but he was deeply interested in receiving my details of overcoming schizophrenia. He expressed delight in being sent a video to hear my story. I told him that it was a homespun effort but nevertheless sought to honour the unbounded possibilities of prayer and glorify the ability of God to answer every need.

"What I say is controversial," I wrote, "to someone like yourself working in the field of psychiatry. But I am sure you will agree, controversial or otherwise, that things have certainly worked out for me after so long, which at the end of the day, so to speak, is all that matters."

I received a wonderfully encouraging letter from him late April 1998 which said:

"I have watched the video with great joy. I am very pleased that you are so well and that you are happily married and enjoying the pleasures of life which in the past were at least partially denied you. Your recovery gives me great pleasure, which I share with you. I would not be so arrogant as to personally claim credit but we doctors are privileged to share the joy of others. The more one studies nature, animals and mankind, the more one is aware of the miraculous quality of what I call 'the machinery'. Increasing knowledge reveals the presence of the Almighty. Orthodox knowledge confirms the presence of the Almighty in the field of mental illness and anguish.

"I wish you all happiness for you and your wife and a continued future of good health."

In a previous conversation, I had told Dr Gittleson of my intention to write my life story in order to give hope to others suffering with schizophrenia. He said he knew of only one other man who had written about coming through schizophrenia and wished me all the best with this endeavour. The business now in hand was to knuckle down and write the details.

14

Further strengthenings of my mind

Since becoming free in 1990, when the power of God healed my psychotic mind, I frequently assessed in the following years if I had fully returned to the strength and freedom I possessed prior to the illness dawning on my life in 1964.

Following the powerful manifestation of the Holy Spirit on freedom day, my mind progressively got stronger as I reclaimed much that had been stolen by demonic powers over 26 years. In 1995, I released a cassette about my healing and concluded by saying that it had taken five years to assume normalcy in the area of mental power and thinking.

I soon realised how much that assessment fell short. Though I progressively got stronger and was greatly restored, a fuller freedom awaited me. As stated in the teachings of Jessie Penn Lewis and Watchman Nee, the return to normal life is gradual and slow, as one is determined to reclaim and possess the areas of life which had been in the grip of evil spirits.

I became stronger through performing two simple acts of faith. Firstly, in claiming protection over my mind and whole life, and through calling out in prayer for more healing strength to be released into my mind. I discovered the paramount importance of continuing cooperation with the Holy Spirit in order to be able to reach full freedom and wholeness.

I came across a helpful prayer of protection in Wesley Duewel's classic book *Mighty Prevailing Prayer*. Through using it constantly, it helped me maintain the freedom and healing. The prayer became etched on my memory …

"But we must by faith appropriate and claim the protection that God has available for us. Claim protection for your body against accident, weakness, and disease. Claim protection for your mind against carelessness, forgetfulness, and all satan's lies and deceptions. Claim protection for your spirit against passivity, indifference, battle weariness, and temptation.

"Claim protection for your work against the onslaughts of satan and his demons through hostile people or circumstances. Claim protection through God's Word, through the blood of the cross, through the name of Jesus. Claim God's wisdom, guidance, and power. Claim the assistance in the invisible of the angel forces of God."

The declaring of this prayer in faith regularly was powerful in preserving what God had achieved, and in strengthening my mind. I believed that successive anointings were available to fortify and build me up.

When I called out for touches of greater power in my mind, knowing God could do far more than I could ever ask or think, He always answered. I was always crying out for these strengthenings, and power flowed into my spirit in discovering more of God.

Throughout 1997 and 1998, I maintained my freedom; but those years contained a lot of weariness in my spirit. I longed to be able to take early retirement and join many more younger than myself wanting a change. At Christmas 1998 I asked about the possibility of being able to look at the terms of an early redundancy package. The details came back in January and were so attractive that I jumped in straight away with both feet to say I would accept them.

To be able to leave work on my 57th birthday on May 11th would be ideal. Staying on afterwards would mean losing a percentage of my pension for each month I remained, so it was important to aim for that date. Now was the right time to make an exit from Royal Mail amidst all the unrest about job security and re-organisation within the business.

I was promised by "the powers that be" that my departure was on the cards and it would happen. I still had to have my annual appraisal assessing performance over the previous year. It gave me great joy to receive a mark of Level 1, the highest grade possible;

something I had never attained before. The icing on the cake, I thought, after over 26 years' service, and just before a promised farewell.

There was something in store that provided an even bigger thrill. It was a greater strengthening by the power of the Holy Spirit during a week's prayer conference held by the Ugandan churches in London. My admiration for the Ugandan prayer leaders first grew when Tina's cousin, Phil Townend from Sowerby Bridge, brought a team of intercessors to our home for a weekend in 1998. They were part of the World Trumpet Mission in Kampala visiting our nation to say thank you for taking the light of the gospel to their country, and were strengthening our hands in prayer.

I had already become linked to a church in Kampala whose leader felt guided to re-visit our country. The conference was something not to be missed, and making the effort to attend was rewarded personally when a Ugandan leader prayed for me. Aaron Mutebi from Entebbe was my partner in a time of interceding for one another. Aaron was no novice in the realm of prayer, having moved into the healing ministry and seen a woman who had been dead for one and half days raised back to life. Her body had been taken into his church at a time the healing service was being held, and Aaron prayed for her not knowing that she was dead.

I simply told him: "Aaron, the Lord has delivered and healed me of schizophrenia, but I have a need for further empowering by the Spirit of God in my mind."

He prayed in his usually powerful way after placing his hand on my head. I then prayed for him, asking God to bless and use him for His glory.

During a sermon, I received a word of guidance about leaving the Lye church. I believed the word was for Tina too. I told her so on the journey home from Heathrow Airport after her trip of encouragement to friends in India. She soon had confirmation, though both of us were a little sad to be leaving the church. We were responding to the guidance of the Holy Spirit and to be obedient was our only concern. We strongly believed there was a spirit of freemasonry at work in the church, causing havoc and spiritual confusion among believers. Until it was recognised by the leadership, no lasting breakthrough could occur.

Confirmation about leaving work finally came through days before my birthday. I was overjoyed in knowing that my request had been granted. I realised on returning to my desk that the jobs I performed as part of the daily routine would soon be coming to an abrupt end. The director over the Security Section offered to pay for the refreshments at my farewell party in recognition of my services to the firm, a gesture deeply appreciated.

Tina in her customary, loving way had arranged for a special cake bearing the Royal Mail logo. She herself was quite at home chatting to my colleagues at my send-off and made the occasion memorable.

Driving away from the office in the car brought mixed emotions. My life was much stronger than in previous years, so I was able to rejoice in bidding farewell to a long career. Quite momentous in one sense to have lasted so long in one job with a condition of schizophrenia which incapacitates many from remaining in any kind of work.

My new-found freedom enabled me to get into action with writing my testimony. I felt it was something crying out to be written. Others like me needed to know the pathway to freedom, and those with relatives suffering schizophrenia needed to hear that God had a way out of the insanity suffered by their loved ones. I didn't give myself any time to enjoy relaxing, though I needed to. I thought of spending about four months finishing the testimony off before I began searching for a part-time job to supplement my pension.

My mind was often tired in recalling and assembling the details of my pathway to freedom and recovery. I thought: 'this is really tiring work,' and I longed to reach the end.

After a long stretch of several months, I began to ease off the pressure. God showed me in prayer that I had been neglecting to seek Him with my whole heart and the writing of the testimony had become too absorbing. My mind needed a hobby, a release so that I would not be too engrossed in the work. So I began to relax more. It was such a refreshing experience that I lost the urgency to get the testimony finished.

But I was quite happy for the temporary abating of flurried activity, knowing that in good time, the zeal and fervour would return, as it indeed did. The advantage of starting up again, though,

had secured a better realisation of the process of recovery, and Tina came to the conclusion that God had done a perfect work of restoration.

To hear her say in February, 2000, that she was now in favour of the testimony going out was a moment of great encouragement. In the past, she had expressed reservations about the writing. She wanted people to see me living normally. In her opinion, people would be impressed that God had done a marvellous work in my life through "just being seen to be normal". It was the full evidence she had always wanted.

She knew me better than anyone, including my mood swings. After a long period of fasting, which opened me up to more of the power of the Holy Spirit, Tina was overjoyed and said: "As far as I am concerned, the testimony can go out now. I feel it is now time to release it for the glory of God and for others to be helped in this difficult area."

In the summer I joined a revolutionary food supplement company. through becoming an independent associate of Mannatech Incorporated, based in Coppel, Texas, which launched into the United Kingdom in November 1999. Mannatech is an amazing functional food research and development company and the world leader in the exciting new field of glyconutritionals.

Tina and I were first told about the company by her cousin, Phil Townend. He and his wife Lynne were thinking about becoming associates themselves and wanted to know our opinions. Among the literature for studying was an impressive letter sent by an Australian pastor, Rod Gilchrist, to 100 church ministers in England drawing attention to the launch in our country. He himself was a leading part-time Presidential in the company in Australia and had already raised large amounts of cash for missions at his church where he was the largest contributor.

I needed a part-time job myself to supplement my pension. I thought that this outlet of encouraging people to take nutritional products to supplement the diet with additional necessary saccharides would provide extra income. Within days, Tina and I had made up our minds to join, and were soon taking regular daily intakes of Mannatech's flagship product, Ambrotose complex.

I longed for my complete testimony to be viewed by someone with psychiatric knowledge and wanted it to be seen and studied by the medically trained. I had often thought of sending my story to the National Schizophrenic Fellowship or the charity SANE: Schizophrenia a National Emergency. At the heart of everything, I wanted God to have the glory for what He had done, and to declare hope for others.

I prayed concerning the release of the testimony and was guided to hold back. This decision was confirmed in the winter of 2002 when engaged in a 37 day fast for prayer breakthrough in our nation. God's invasion of inner liberty dealt with even more issues relating to my past life, and at the time was a wonderful surprise.

It proved to be another breakthrough into freedom which I felt was the "final touch" in the area of restoration. I knew God had broken through yet again in a more significant way, as if adding to an ever-increasing freedom. The discipline of the fast had been difficult sometimes to carry out in the home but through persevering, breakthrough resulted.

What God achieved was confirmed when a new Ugandan pastor had a most unusual dream the first night he stayed at our home. Pastor Aloysius Kizza described it:

"At night before I slept I felt oppressed and sleepless. I entered spiritual warfare and began to sprinkle the blood of Jesus in the whole house, then eventually I fell asleep.

"A very big and long python snake had been killed by somebody I did not know. I was supposed to remove its skin. I felt I must cut off the head before removing the skin. I had a panga in my right hand. As I tried to cut off the head, the white stuff (poison) came out and was looking funny and scaring. I found it difficult to cut it off completely. Somebody came and stood behind me who I did not recognise and asked to help me.

"He held my hand and cut off the head completely. It was now ready to be skinned. And I heard a voice saying, 'the giant is slain', and woke up from the sleep. I sensed that the person who held my hand and helped me cut off the head was either the Angel or the Lord Jesus Himself. Then there was a great sense of victory and peace in my spirit."

It was not long before I realised that the giant who had been slain was the demonic force of evil that had held me captive for 26 years. I rejoiced at this confirmation of the perfect work of salvation and deliverance by Jesus Christ my Saviour. In the summer, it was one of the happiest moments of my life to be able to travel to Uganda and testify of God's delivering and healing power. Never before had I faced such a responsive congregation. People with bondages rooted in witchcraft, tribalism and other satanic influences understood what I was talking about.

I believed the ministry there was the forerunner of much more to come.

15

Why did it take so long?

"**G**od gets His greatest victories out of apparent defeats," says the
first sentence of the January 18th meditation of *Streams in the
Desert*, the spiritual classic by Mrs C E Cowman, a daily reading I
rejoiced over less than four months away from my 55th birthday.

It brought so much inspiration and encouragement with its
spiritual insight that out of it came this chapter. Some may ask:
"Why did God allow you to go through such affliction and be
tempest-tossed for 26 years? Why did He delay helping you for so
long? If, as you say, He is a God of love, then why didn't He move
in earlier and lead you out?" Questions for which I have sought
answers through prayer and reading the Bible, but they no longer
pose a problem. Before dealing with them, let me refer to diary
entries made on the morning I read the meditation.

"The time is 9.50 on a Saturday, and I have been moving around
since 5.30 trying to press ahead writing my story to bring hope to
others. After a busy working week and a prayer night commitment
at church in mid-week, I still felt tired at 7 a.m. so went back to bed
for a couple of hours.

"Finding these days the ability to pull myself away from work
when tired, a discipline not found easy since deliverance, I rested on
the bed and turned to this reading which inspired me to begin writing

"I thought about 26 years of bondage and the fact, well known to
the medical profession, that a person my age goes deeper and deeper
into the illness of schizophrenia, and is, therefore, unlikely to break
free of it. I then read the following lines with great joy: 'Very often

the enemy seems to triumph for a little [and in my case for a very long time] and God lets it be so; but then He comes in and upsets all the work of the enemy, overthrows the apparent victory, and as the Bible says, "turns the way of the wicked upside down." '

"And when it continued, 'Thus He gives a great deal larger victory than we would have known if He had not allowed the enemy, seemingly, to triumph in the first place,' I just knew that Jesus Christ was re-emphasising the fact that He achieved greater things because of the tremendous victory secured in my life after so very, very long.

"My heart welled up with praise to God that He could not only get great honour from my life by having delivered and healed me, but obtain much more by having done it after so many years. In this showing not only His power to deliver, but His commitment to give strength to those who surrender their lives to Him."

I then found a fuller, wonderful expansion of God's dealings. I continued to read the meditation quoting from the section "Life of Praise", the story of the three Hebrew youths being thrown into the fiery furnace:

"Here was an apparent victory for the enemy. It looked as if the servants of the living God were going to have a terrible defeat. We have all been in places where it seemed as though we were defeated, and the enemy rejoiced. We can imagine what a complete defeat this looked to be. They fell down into the flames, and their enemies watched them to see them burn up in that awful fire, but were greatly astonished to see them walking around in the fire enjoying themselves.

"King Nebuchadnezzar told them to 'come forth out of the midst of the fire' [Daniel 3: 26 KJV]. Not even a hair was singed, nor was the smell of fire on their garments, 'because there is no other god that can deliver after this sort'. This apparent defeat resulted in a marvellous victory. Suppose that these three men had lost their faith and courage, and had complained, saying, 'Why did not God keep us out of the furnace!' They would have been burned, and God would not have been glorified. If there is a great trial in your life today, do not own it as a defeat, but continue, by faith, to claim the victory through Him who is able to make you more than conqueror, and a glorious victory will soon be apparent."

I put the book down again, and worshipped God. More than at any other time since deliverance day in 1990 I saw that in His dealings with men and women, God is seeking to bring great glory to His name through our lives. If He chooses to delay opening a prison door to freedom for a long time in order to magnify the keeping power of His faithfulness and love, my privilege is to agree and join His purposes for my life. Here was ample and convincing proof that He not only saved me as a teenager, but also kept me for an extraordinary length of time through His power when life knew only struggle and battle for survival.

I just stayed in that moment on my bed weeping tears of gratitude before such a wonderful God and Saviour. I knew that the business in hand was to get it down before any other part of the testimony I was writing.

Tina was tidying up the bedroom, and I stopped her on the landing.

Putting my arms around her, I said, "I've just had a word from the Lord. That as there was no trace of Shadrach, Meshach and Abednego having smoke on their garments, or of having their hair singed, so there will be no trace of my mind suffering the years of schizophrenia."

The previous night we had enjoyed the late night film, "The Preacher's Wife", starring Whitney Houston. Having arrived home about 11 p.m., a time that would normally have caused panic attacks concerning the fear of my not being rested enough for the following day, I added jokingly: "I'll soon be taking you to the midnight movie!"

I thought of the ways in which God was being glorified through what He had done and was still doing for me. My thoughts flashed first to a friend who recently told me she kept listening to the audio cassette of my testimony to inspire her own condition with hope. She lost her daughter tragically at a time she desperately needed medical help.

And then my mind went to the words of St Paul writing in 2 Corinthians, chapter 1: "Praise be to the God and Father of our Lord Jesus Christ, the Father of compassion and the God of all comfort, who comforts us in all our troubles, so that we can comfort those in any trouble with the comfort we ourselves have received from God."

Meditating on those words I said to Maurice, aged 83, who had just returned from a prayer meeting at church: "D'you know, I've just had another reason why our testimony is not our own, but the Lord's. For in telling others what Christ has done for us, we are saying He can do the same for them. If Christ has brought us through suffering, we can offer hope to others that Jesus can bring them through too."

He replied: "What a wonderful Saviour is Jesus my Lord."

I pondered on the number of Christians I knew or heard of with varying kinds of mental bondage suggestive of the great area where real hope of freedom is needed. Others too, who though not subject to this most severe form of psychological incarceration are always living under something which prevents them from breaking into real freedom. So many Christians are tied up with a kind of captivity in their lives which the power of Jesus is well able to break and triumph over through His resurrection life!

I thought, too, of the young man outside the Royal Mail office in Sheffield who showed schizophrenic symptoms. He used to stand at the bus stop and found his pleasure in making the sound of a bus as one approached while at the same time trying to make visual contact with the driver.

Then there was the man in his early thirties I just happened to meet outside the office when I transferred to Birmingham. He had nowhere to sleep and used to carry a polythene bag filled with "bubble packaging". A man in great need, known to the police with schizophrenic patterns, who wore inadequate clothing in winter months. So withdrawn and full of fear inside his own world that an offer of a warm coat was refused because of his inability to accept it.

I later thought of the time shortly after being delivered and healed when a friend had prophesied over me, declaring that "God is going to restore the years the locusts have eaten and go on to make your life a blessing in His hands."

It was a tremendous encouragement to hear that, bearing in mind that through the 26 years of struggle and bondage I had always maintained a desire to serve and glorify God. Pondering the prophecy filled me with immense joy and anticipation. I had been aware during those years that my mental problem had been a barrier to my being accepted in interviews for pastorates in the Assemblies

of God and also at London City Mission. But at the same time I had a question in my heart to raise before the Lord.

While not doubting the Lord's ability to accomplish what He had said in the prophecy concerning restoring the years the locusts had eaten, I asked the question, "Well, Lord, how are you going to do that? Twenty-six years is a long time out of a person's life."

Then I found myself providing my own answer as certain Scriptures came to mind. "Jim," I told myself, "you're thinking as a human. God's ways are higher than your ways and He can do whatever He says. With Him a day is as a thousand years and a thousand years as a day, and He can so fill your remaining days and years by just doing what He says. Without a doubt, I shall know He has restored the years of suffering."

Desirous of looking a little closer at the context in which the words "restoring the years the locusts have eaten" occur, I went to the word of God to see how He had fulfilled what He had said to the children of Israel.

I took time to think of the "great high notes of praise that God could receive" through His faithful dealings with me. How interested people would be in believing in such a God of love who was so committed not only to keep me in the midst of such a hellish bondage but so arrange the circumstances of my life to bring me out into freedom. What a revelation to Christians and non-Christians concerning the power of prayer!

The human interest side to the story was also captivating. The account of how God had arranged heaven-sent love matches of two wives, who were without doubt His choice provision, was immensely fascinating. Having worked as a journalist gave me a good idea of the kind of story which soaks up interest. Love stories always have an audience, and mine was indeed an exceptional love story — but all arranged by a God of love working by selecting for me the ideal partner on two occasions.

God is simply wonderful in His overall and complete care of His children. I never doubt that God loves me. When I contemplate how He brought Pam into my life at a time of desperate need and guided her into marriage, knowing that I had schizophrenia, I continue to be amazed.

Married to such a wife, who loved me through 14 years, even

though the last three and a half were for her a time of great testing and difficulty because of the cancer, fills me with untold gratitude and worship. Many women in these days would no doubt have walked out in a short space of time; but Pam was the exceptional kind — completely devoted to her Lord and also to me in her love and care.

Because I was always preoccupied with life inside my schizophrenic prison, I had no appreciation of the immense patience she had in bearing with my mental weaknesses. She certainly endured all things with the love of Christ reigning in her life in respect of my many shortcomings. Her faith was strong and unswerving with a Christ-likeness that endeared her to believers and unbelievers alike. There were many times when she was cast upon the Lord she loved, bearing the responsibility for the most part of caring for our children.

She must have longed many times to see a breakthrough of freedom in my life as she battled on perseveringly and patiently, seeing the marriage vow as honouring to God.

Then there was the time when I received news of her cancer, and I can clearly recall how devastated I was. Whenever I am asked what has Jesus done for me, I have more to tell than what may be termed a "normal testimony" of having been saved from my sin. God kept me faithful to Him through 26 years of hell in a prison house of schizophrenia in spite of the added pressure, unbearable at times, of knowing my wife had terminal cancer.

Many stories appear in magazines about a husband or wife having coped with a partner passing through trying and difficult times because of their terminal illness. How much more glory does my Saviour receive in that He brought me safely through that experience while living inside the most severe mental prison house of life itself.

A personal friend confided in me at a time when his wife was in hospital and things were uncertain about her condition:

"I don't know how I would cope if I were to lose her. I can't imagine how I would carry on."

I liken that experience to having been thrown into the furnace of life's pressures where the heat was turned up to what may be considered to be intolerable odds BUT GOD was there with me in

the midst.

I then considered the years after Pam's death, which, but for the grace and faithfulness of God, could well have been "drop-out years". The struggle to come to terms with her passing; the trauma and shock adding themselves to my schizophrenic condition; further visits to the psychiatric hospital; the feeling of utter abandonment followed by strong satanic pressure seeking to destroy me — all met by the power of God standing with me.

Life after Pam's death was devastating and difficult — until along came Tina, God's sweetheart number two; brought into my life through a Christian dating agency. Many Christians frown at the thought of ever being able to secure a match by such means. They doubt how God can use this so-called "unusual avenue" for providing the perfect partner. However, He did it for me that way. Somehow Tina was inspired to do what she would not normally do in travelling 70 miles or so to look me over.

I stand amazed at the intervention and planning of God, absolutely amazed. I tell myself over and over again: "Never lose sight of all she endured to pull you through, and remember the vision, without which you would have let her go on the day she wanted to finish. Keep in mind, too, the prayer backup of Maurice and Esther and many others who were included in God's plan of getting me free."

I never knew the interpretation of the phrase "God's silent years" in the life of a believer until this period in my life. Years in which nothing seemed to be happening. My years were years of struggling to survive, but the silence I refer to is the lack of God moving in and doing something. It's only after you have come through such an experience that you know God was "in it" with you. All the time He was preserving, strengthening and keeping me alive.

Many instances come to mind of how the Lord helped in life's circumstances, as He used them as stepping-stones on the way to freedom. To the question: "Why did it take so long?" I have found one more satisfying explanation in the matter of enduring affliction, even though caused by a demonic presence. Having come through searching fires of deep soul-anguish over 26 years, today I know God deeper than at any other time in my life. I once prayed, "I don't care what it costs, Lord, I want to know You better."

Most likely in answer to that prayer, God was with me in the furnace of pain and sustained me there for so long. If by calling on His grace in it all, I have come to know Him more, and if by allowing Him to display His faithfulness and power through me others are drawn to God, then what better reason is there for having submitted to His will. God be praised!

16

There is hope for the schizophrenic

Nothing receives more attention in our modern society than the area of the human mind. Because of the increased incidence of insanity affecting countless numbers, there never was a more urgent time for people to receive the power of the risen Lord Jesus Christ to transform their besieged and distressed lives.

It is not only those labelled psychiatric patients who are being affected by satanic powers. People from every walk of life, religion and culture across the length and breadth of our ever-shrinking world are being impacted in their minds by the pressures of spiritual darkness robbing them of precious sanity itself.

I ask: Is there hope for the mentally disturbed? Can the ever-increasing number of charities brought into being offer a glimmer of real hope to sufferers who daily face a satanic blanket of darkness over life? Can anything be done for the helpless and seemingly hopeless case of the schizophrenic let loose into society whom no one understands or cares for?

There is hope for the mentally sick, mentally disturbed, mentally assailed or mentally battered and bruised in modern life. Hope which releases freedom and wholeness promised by Jesus Christ, the Son of the eternal God, through His death and resurrection in Jerusalem 2,000 years ago. Hope, yes, real hope, in Him but in no other. I have proved that fact in my own life. You've read my story and ought to be asking: "What can believing prayer in Jesus Christ do for me?"

True, Jesus is the only answer for the problem of sin in every life. How important it is to know the peace of mind and heart that He brings. Because He is the one and only true God, He can do the

impossible. He obtained for us the power of the Holy Spirit to live a Christ-centred and victorious life — but the receiving of that power and His resources are conditional. Everything hinges on receiving Him as Lord and Saviour through faith and acknowledging His sacrifice on the cross at Calvary as the only effective sacrifice procuring your eternal salvation.

In saying a schizophrenic COULD be healed and delivered, the declaration has to be qualified. A schizophrenic must see the importance of receiving Christ by faith into his heart despite the turmoil in his or her mind. Believing the controversial but spiritually discerned conviction that schizophrenia is not in the genes but can have its roots in demonic activity, it would be needful for a person to receive Christ for reasons of their own safety.

Jesus Himself pointed to the need of protection in Matthew 12: 43-45 where He says: "When an evil spirit comes out of a man, it goes through arid places, seeking rest, and does not find it. Then it says, 'I will return to the house I left.' When it arrives, it finds the house unoccupied, swept clean and put in order.

"Then it goes and takes with it seven other spirits more wicked than itself, and they go in and live there. And the final condition of that man is worse than the first. That is how it will be with this wicked generation."

What Jesus says here in effect is that after a person is delivered of demon spirits, the Holy Spirit needs to fill the area they have vacated. If that doesn't happen, then that person is in very great danger of finishing up worse than the previous condition. Only the power of the Holy Spirit would keep at bay the same demon returning with seven other spirits worse than the first.

Such a person would need God to help sort his/her life out. It would only be possible with the power of the Holy Spirit. Compassionate and Holy Spirit-led Christians would need to be found to offer love and prayer support, and it would be no short-term commitment. The reason is that the person would have to start living in two new relationships: seeing and knowing himself after being set free, with the additional experience of beginning a new life with Christ. With Christ helping, teaching and guiding that person he could hope to be restored to normal life. Yes, a living relationship with Christ could do it.

As my testimony has shown, I had the presence of the Holy Spirit in my life before my illness went into full bloom in my early twenties. Without that power I would have been unable to fight the evil presence of schizophrenia. I also had a tremendously long period after healing and deliverance had taken place to allow myself to "catch up" on 26 years in which I had not developed and grown normally. But God did it! The years after healing and deliverance were times of slow but definite progress, requiring most of all a dependency on the Holy Spirit to teach, correct, inspire and show me those things I needed to know. I needed Tina's help too, and the prayers of friends, to get me there.

Since becoming free, I have reflected that although the 26 years were watched over by the faithfulness and love of God, those years for me were in a very real sense "absent" years. Years of not being aware of growing up in my early twenties, unaware that there were more things needing doing for my children apart from being their friend. Unable to do things like sport that I used to enjoy, and never having the strength to do my work and know fulfilment in it, instead of struggling. There was a long gap in my life which made it difficult to believe my age was almost 48 on deliverance day. During the subsequent years when people asked: "And when do you retire, Jim?" I couldn't get my head round that one. In age I felt that I was still somewhere back in my twenties.

Bearing in mind that God knew what He was doing, I have come to accept that the "gap" years referred to were not without significance because God was filling that time by faithfully watching over me, strengthening me and showing His commitment of never-failing love. I trust that many who have read my testimony will realise and rejoice that He never wavers and His power and love are sufficient to bring deliverance, freedom and healing.

Restoration to full wholeness will require a determined and definite cooperation by any Christian who suffered schizophrenia after first coming to Christ. So if it is going to be a hard battle for anyone already a Christian before the illness dawns, how much more so for someone who, as a schizophrenic, receives Christ.

It is encouraging to see the amount of effort the Christian Church in our land is making to lead people with mental problems into freedom. Many, while desirous of following Christ, are held

back because of generational curses affecting their lives. Bondages going back three and four generations run riot in lives today and need dealing with. But despite the signs of getting involved with the mentally ill, much more needs to be done by the Church in this area.

To care for the mentally sick and love them with the compassion of Jesus is not the glamorous kind of Christian evangelism that may win us a name or recognition, but God notices when we move out in His Name to love, care and bring deliverance.

Every time I hear of a killing done by a schizophrenic, my heart goes out to him in his sickness. High profile incidents such as the murder by a schizophrenic of a social worker while visiting a hostel for the mentally ill in Balham, south London, and his subsequent conviction are becoming regular news items. This man was said to suffer from an "untreatable personality disorder". I suggest they present a challenge to the Christian Church to get its hands dirty and its heart engaged in offering Christ's compassion and delivering power for such hopeless cases.

That is why I want to do my part in declaring His love and power through PUSH — Prayer Until Schizophrenia Heals — and with a trumpet voice declare that Jesus Christ is the only answer and hope for so many lives held in the grip of a bondage so powerful.

The offer of the love and power of Jesus is so relevant today for everyone. Every Christian knows he faces the implacable hate and serpentine subtlety of our adversary the devil and makes it the business of the day to stand fast against him while advancing the kingdom of God. To liberate untold numbers whose minds are captive, teach them the power of the word of God and life lived in the spirit of prayer is gloriously possible.

Nothing is too difficult for God!!

I do not understand the nature of the research being carried out into schizophrenia in attempts to reach a solution to this complex mental illness. I wish those engaged in this work every success in trying to solve what is a most baffling problem. It would be a breakthrough to understand why a person can live normally up to or just beyond teenage years before the "dawn of devastation" changes life completely. To understand why this latent force within a person

bursts forth would answer many heart-searching questions.

But there is another focus of importance which must be entered into, namely, that of praying to seek God for insight into the darkness. For plainly it is an illness which not only demands the former kind of investigation but also the kind which calls or cries out to the Almighty God, the Creator of the human body. Living in a fallen world it is of utmost importance to consult the living God, who through Jesus Christ came to undo and conquer every realm of life affected by sin, of which schizophrenia is part.

I find it quite amazing that in my struggle over such a long period of time, the only help I was given came in tablet or injection form, aimed at containing the illness. It was not until the desire to become free grew in my spirit through the inspiration of the Holy Spirit that God gradually began to unfold the steps leading to deliverance. Already, as with everything else, God knew the way out of this embroiled and compounded maze of a problem with its stronghold wrapped solidly around my mind. He had already made available to me through His death and resurrection the same power that raised Him from the dead.

My story seeks to give the due honour and glory to God's ability to solve the impossible. "The possibilities of prayer are established by the facts and the history of prayer. Facts are stubborn things. Facts are the true things. They cannot be ignored", wrote a mighty intercessor.

The evil power in my life was definitely demonic; there is ample evidence of that. It is interesting to debate the roots of schizophrenia but far more interesting to be honest in acknowledging the obvious present devastation it causes. Plainly, those held in its grip lack the normal freedom enjoyed by everyone else. It may be profitable to argue about the source of the psychotic disorder — to ask: does the illness start from cells disturbed in the womb, or, as some suggest, is the origin in the expectant mother contracting some sickness or, as I believe, is it rooted in a demon of rejection — but without doubt demons can thereby find an easy entry point into the human body to make it their home.

I know of no other way for schizophrenia to be defeated but by using the power of prayer in the name of Jesus Christ of Nazareth, the Son of God, and applying the authority of the blood of Jesus shed

at Calvary. Until there is recognition of the satanic powers behind the condition — leave behind the argument if you will of the source, and concentrate on the plight of every schizophrenic sufferer shackled in bondage — and a determination to deal with it, I see little hope of freedom being found and the condition overcome.

However, as detailed in my account, there is hope in God for deliverance. I believe that through the death of Christ on the cross, forgiveness and restoration may be received and His wonderful indwelling life enjoyed. God is still able to deliver and heal all sorts and conditions of people — something which is powerfully amazing. When I look at His ability to restore a schizophrenic, as He has done for me, I doubly marvel at the wonderful power of God.

What a mighty Saviour He is! A powerful Redeemer who came to destroy the works of satan in every form. I recommend Him to you. He's well worth knowing!!

Recommended for further reading:

God and Healing of the Mind   Trevor Dearing

Total Healing   Trevor Dearing

The God of Miracles   Trevor and Anne Dearing

These are published by Crossbridge Books.

CPSIA information can be obtained
at www.ICGtesting.com
Printed in the USA
LVHW081304290119
605649LV00014B/158/P

9 780954 357344